Practical Duct Tape Projects

Practical Duct Tape Projects

Instructables.com

Edited and Introduced by
Noah Weinstein

Skyhorse Publishing

Skyhorse Publishing books may be purchased in bulk at special discounts for sales promotion, corporate gifts, fund-raising, or educational purposes. Special editions can also be created to specifications. For details, contact the Special Sales Department, Skyhorse Publishing, 307 West 36th Street, 11th Floor, New York, NY 10018 or info@skyhorsepublishing.com.

Skyhorse® and Skyhorse Publishing® are registered trademarks of Skyhorse Publishing, Inc.®, a Delaware corporation.

Visit our website at www.skyhorsepublishing.com.

10 9 8 7 6 5 4 3 2 1

Library of Congress Cataloging-in-Publication Data is available on file.

ISBN: 978-1-62087-709-8

Printed in China

Disclaimer:

This book is intended to offer general guidance. It is sold with the understanding that every effort was made to provide the most current and accurate information. However, errors and omissions are still possible. Any use or misuse of the information contained herein is solely the responsibility of the user, and the author and publisher make no warrantees or claims as to the truth or validity of the information. The author and publisher shall have neither liability nor responsibility to any person or entity with respect to any loss or damage caused, or alleged to have been caused, directly or indirectly, by the information contained in this book. Furthermore, this book is not intended to give professional dietary, technical, or medical advice. Please refer to and follow any local laws when using any of the information contained herein, and act responsibly and safely at all times.

Table of Contents

table of contents

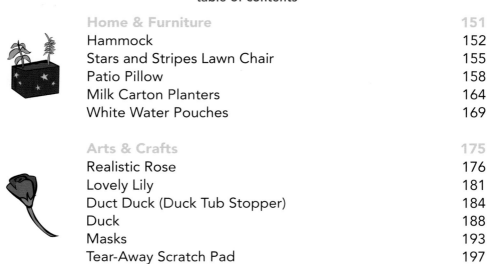

Introduction

The creators of these whimsical projects have re-engineered the practical elements of the world around them, solely out of duct tape. While not perhaps your most common of building mediums, duct tape is a versatile, low-cost building platform that has its own distinct advantages. Not only is duct tape cheap, durable, self-adhering, removable, and waterproof, it also comes in every color from standard gray to leopard print. Duct tape can be used to make unique bags, wallets, totes, apparel, decorations, and even furnishings. Each project contains multiple images with step-by-step instructions to help you create one of these duct tape masterpieces, or to inspire you to make and share a duct tape creation of your own.

All of the projects in this book are from Instructables.com. Instructables is the most popular project-sharing community on the Internet, and part of the Autodesk family of creative communities. Since August 2005, Instructables has provided easy publishing tools to enable passionate, creative people to share their most innovative projects, recipes, skills, and ideas. Instructables has over 80,000 projects covering all subjects, including crafts, art, electronics, kids, home improvement, pets, outdoors, reuse, bikes, cars, robotics, food, decorating, woodworking games, and more.

(Mask on page 193.)

* Special thanks to Instructables Interactive Designer Gary Lu for the Instructables Robot illustrations!

Section 1
Bags & Totes

Messenger Bag and Hardware

By neumaics
http://www.instructables.com/
id/Duct-Tape-Messenger-
Bag-Hardware/

This Instructable completely details the construction of a duct tape messenger bag. This includes the bag structure and hardware to make it useful. It can be made and ready to use within a few hours. No stitching is required. Other than the metal pieces used in the hardware, it is made completely with duct tape. Total construction time is about two hours.

I have been using a prototype as often as practical for school and it has performed admirably—with a few flaws. It took a few weeks to recognize and repair most of the weaknesses and has operated stress free for most of the semester. It's also survived a couple of semi-rigorous bike rides.

This tutorial is based on the bag I've been using, but with important changes that will improve durability. Also, this is the most basic design I've made. Version 2 can be easily customized to suit the needs of the builder.

Here are pictures of the model currently in use (v2.2) and the one made for this Instructable. Version 2.2 has taken some abuse and has undergone many, many repairs.

Don't let the nineteen steps daunt you—making a messenger bag from scratch can become complex. I've attempted to simplify the process as much as possible.

Step 1: Gather Materials

Materials you need for the bag structure

1. Duct tape—three 30 yd rolls
2. Scissors
3. Cutting board
4. Pins
5. Yard stick

I imagine any brand or color of duct tape will do. For this Instructable and my previous bags, I used standard Scotch/3M brand tape. It is 1.88" wide, gray, and purchased at the local hardware store. For your first go at this, I suggest whatever is least expensive. The scissors, cutting board, and pins can be purchased from any sewing supply store. If you don't want to pay for a cutting board, it can be substituted for a flat sheet of corrugated card board that has linear dimensions more than 3' × 3'. I haven't tried it this way, but it should work. Also the pins can be substituted for thumb tacks—you'll need 44 at the very least. If you sew, you probably have good scissors, a cutting board, and pins readily available. Please note: Don't use your good scissors and pins to do this Instructable.* They will become gunky from the duct tape's sticky substance and annoying to use later on. I suggest that, after using pins for the first run, you separate them from your other sewing pins. Use a less-loved pair of scissors if you can. After cutting a few pieces of duct tape, your scissors will gunk up and cutting performance/quality will diminish greatly. It is worth the time to take a moment to clean gunk off of the scissors so they can cut cleanly again.

Materials needed to construct the hardware

1. Duct tape
2. Marker flags
3. Tension pins
4. Washers
5. Pliers
6. Tin snips
7. Sacrificial ruler
8. Regular ruler

This portion is optional! If you have hardware lying around, you can easily use that. I don't recommend it though. All materials can be bought at Home Depot, except for the ruler maybe.

Hardware includes handle anchors,  shoulder strap anchors, and buckles. As mentioned, you can salvage these from another, preferably useless, bag. I strongly suggest that you don't ruin a perfectly useful bag just to make a mostly useful bag. That would be silly. Amounts of different materials will be discussed in the hardware portion (step 12).

After gathering materials to build the bag structure, you may move to the next step without fear of injury.

*You can periodically clean the scissors or pins with eucalyptus oil or goo remover. Be careful when cleaning scissors with plastic parts, as goo could dissolve these parts.

Step 2: Understand the Plan

Duct tape is frustrating to manipulate in long lengths. You can

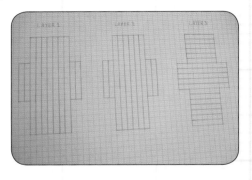

easily degrade the quality of the bag—if not completely ruin your work—if you mess up even once. Therefore I highly suggest you understand the plan of action before starting. Of course you can skip through the steps and learn that way, but I have them condensed conveniently on this one page. Simply, we will build layers of tape sheets that will form a flat shell, which we will fold into a useful, bag-like shape. The areas that comprise the panels of the bag are marked on the first picture. The outside border serves as an interface between the panels and also helps make a clean edge when finishing. The second picture shows the layers we will be making. Although three are shown, there will be five in this tutorial. The other two are permutations on the other three and optional, though recommended. Notice how layer two is only ten widths wide rather than eleven widths wide for layer one? This is how we get the border on the left and right sides of the sheet—layer two is offset by .94" on either side. It seems simple . . . and it is! In practice, though, there are annoying bits due to the nature of sticky back tape. Now that you understand the project completely, we can proceed.

Step 3: Begin Layer One

Here we begin in the logical place. After components are gathered, find an open area free of wandering animals or children. Spread the cutting board/cardboard over a large, flat surface. Make the duct tape, pins, and scissors handy. Cut one 36" strip of duct tape. With the sticky side face up, pin a corner to the board. Make sure you will have enough room on either side to accommodate the full width of the sheet. Pull the opposite corner of the pinned corner taught and pin. Make sure the length of the tape is as a straight as possible. Finish pinning the other corners, and adjust geometry as necessary. Repeat six more times. Try to minimize the gap between the lengths, of course keeping the length as straight as possible. Layer one is not done—it still needs side panels, but we'll get back to finishing it in a few steps.

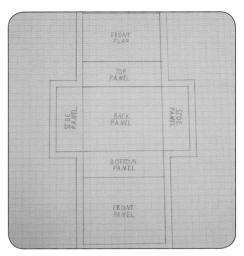

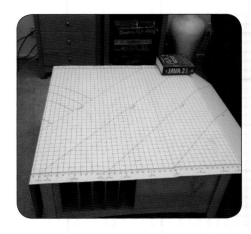

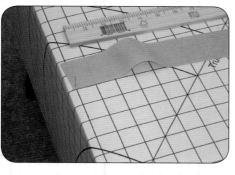

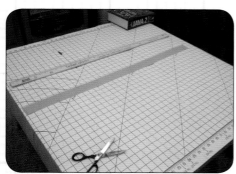

Step 4: Begin Layer Two

Layer two begins much like layer one. There are no pins this time. Cut a 35" length of duct tape and place about 1" offset of the first layer. This operation takes practice, you'll find. I suggest you stand or sit perpendicular to the sheet of tape. After cutting the 35" piece of tape, stick your right thumb and middle finger to the corners on the right of the tape, doing likewise with your left hand. After both sides are stuck securely to your two fingers, pull taught. Align the piece above where it needs to be placed and slowly lower, adjusting as necessary. Lower until the piece is attached to the first layer. If you make a mistake, try to minimize the amount of contact with the bottom layer and pull it gently off, then try again. You may accidentally pull the first layer up while pulling up on a failed strip placement. If this happens, just re-seat the pins, while making sure that the strip of tape is still aligned. Repeat five more times, and you're done with the first tricky part.

Step 5: Begin Layer Three

If you had trouble with the previous step, the next part should be much easier. Cut six pieces of tape 11.25" long. Using the same thumb/middle finger technique as before, place this layer perpendicular to the previous layers at the "top" of the sheet. These pieces should span the second layer, covering it completely. Place all six pieces. Then we can move onto finishing the first and second layer.

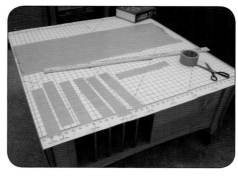

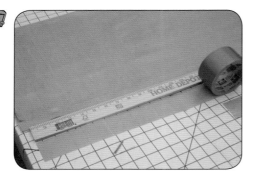

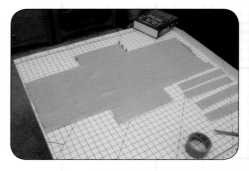

Step 6: Finish Layer One and Layer Two

Layer one and layer two require the side panels to be added. Rather than wasting duct tape, or measuring where the tape might fall, I use this method because it shows exactly where the side panels need to be. Begin by cutting four more 11.25" strips of tape. Place two on either side. Using the same pinning method as in layer one, pin the strips to the sides so that the top of the tape is parallel with the middle of the last piece of layer three placed. Pin all four pieces that comprise your side panels, then move on. Layer two is finished by cutting four 11" strips of tape and placing them on top of the newly finished layer one, except with roughly 1" offset. If there is any confusion, I suggest you look at the diagram. After the side panels are completed, you can move on to finish layer three.

Step 7: Finish Layer Three

Layer three restarts where we left off, naturally. To finish it, we will need to cover the new side panels. This will take five 19" strips of tape (actually 18.8", if you can measure/cut that accurately). Again, this is only to cover layer two, which may or may not be 19" wide. The first picture shows how to eyeball the measurement. It turns out that it's close enough to 19" and this wasn't necessary. Place these butted against the previously placed strips of tape in layer three. Cut seven more 11.25" pieces of tape and continue to place below the 19" lengths. Layers 1–3 are now finished! Continue with layer four.

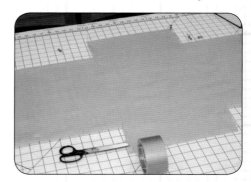

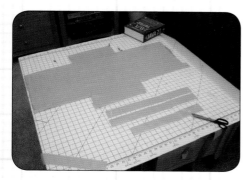

three. After placing all 11.25" pieces of tape, cut five 19" strips of tape and place those as you did with the previous strips.

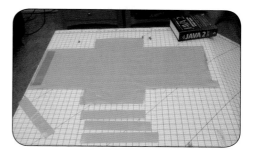

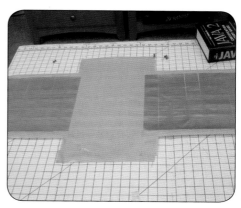

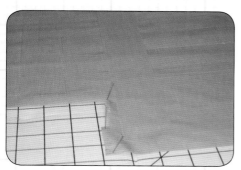

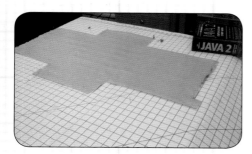

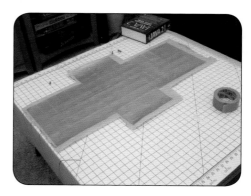

Step 8: Layer Four

Layer four is exactly like layer three, except that the sticky side is down. Be aware, once a strip of layer four is placed, it cannot be removed without causing damage to the lower layers. Fortunately, finding where to place the strips of tape is easy. Small gaps are acceptable, but try to stay consistent with layer three and try not to get too far off. Begin as you did with layer three. Cut six 11.25" strips of tape. Place the sticky side down on top of layer three. Cut seven more 11.25" pieces. Place sticky side down directly above the seven non-covered 11.25" strips of layer

Step 9: Layer Five

Layer five is the easiest of the layers. Furthermore, it is optional, though I would recommend it. It's similar to layer two, except where the side panels are concerned. The side panel strips of tape in layer five only cover layer two, three, and four—try not to touch layer one with

7

layer five. It's also easy . . . so go at it. The pictures don't capture how easy it happens to be. They also don't capture too much detail with the compression, but trust me; there are more differences between the pictures than placement of scissors. At this point, you can unpin the sheet and admire your work (carefully placing the pins in a container while you're at it—no one likes stepping on pins). Be careful to keep the outer border clean—it will form the basis of the bag structure and nicely finished edges.

Step 10: Fold the Sheet into a Bag

We've arrived at the most annoying, yet one of the most important steps: folding the sheet into a bag. First, trim all edges to be about 0.7" all around. That's an arbitrary number—just make sure that the outer edges are mostly consistent. Be sure to cut off any needle holes. You also need to cut a 45 degree slice where the sides fold in on the corner. The top-left one is labeled, but the other three need to be cut as well. After the edges are all trimmed, we can begin folding. We are going to mate sticky border to sticky border. First, mate the side panels to the bottom, then the front panel to the side panels. If you mess up, that is okay. Try to limit contact of the sticky border until you are certain that is how you want it positioned. If you must retry, you can try pulling the connected pieces apart, then attempt to rejoin them. If some of the sticky parts come off, that is okay, too—just keep trying. If you completely destroy the sticky part and are beginning to damage the fabric of the bag, then I suggest you trim the destroyed bit of layer one and use additional tape to reinforce the seam. Any ugliness will be covered up in the next step (cleanup).

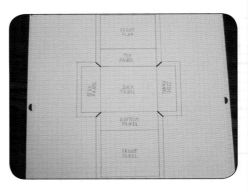

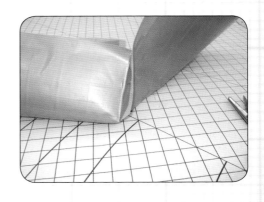

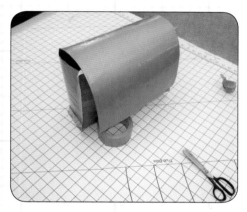

Step 11: Clean the Bag

Here we mean "clean" so as to make the appearance more presentable. In this step, you actually cannot use too much duct tape. Seriously, you can go crazy if you want. Also, the length of the tape isn't so important—it just needs to be long enough. I'm going to try to make this bag look clean and symmetrical, but you can make it look how you want, of course. I have detailed in this step what I believe to be the very minimum cleaning before moving onto the hardware. There is no order to this step that needs to be followed—just tape the interface border to the bag, reinforce the inside seams, and cover any other exposed seams. I also suggest covering all corners in the end. If you haven't done so already, you can fold the border into the top panel and front flap.

Step 12: Gather Materials for the Hardware

I split the hardware into three segments: the handle anchors, the shoulder strap anchors, and the front flap buckle. Notes: Most parts can be bought at Home Depot. I was unable to find 5/16" × 1/2" tension pins there, but the other ones mentioned are sold, though quantities are limited. The marker flags come in packs of 100. You'll only need two for all the hardware in this Instructable, at most, but I'm sure you can find a use for the remaining 98. McMaster-Carr sells everything you will need (and probably a lot more you don't need).

For the handle, you will need

1. Duct tape
2. Four 5/16" × 1" tension pins
3. One marker flag
4. "Structural bar" (see note below)
5. Scissors
6. Pliers
7. Tin snips
8. Permanent marker

The "structural bar" used in this bag is an aluminum ruler. You can use the free paint stirrers, other flat bits of metal, or just about anything small, flat, and rigid.

For the shoulder straps, you will need:
1. Duct tape
2. Four 5/16" × 2" tension pins
3. One marker flag
4. All tools mentioned above

For the front flap buckle, you will need
1. Duct tape
2. Three 5/16" × 1" tension pins
3. Two 5/16" × 1/2" tension pins
4. One marker flag
5. Two or more #10 washers
6. All tools mentioned above
7. Cross-cut metal-working file (Optional; . . . or you can use some hook-and-loop fasteners (Velcro) to secure the front flap.)

All the parts are very similar, so I detailed the bending of only one. The pictures are more descriptive than I can be, so I suggest you examine them closely. Once you've decided what you want to make, you can move forward, prepared.

Step 13: Make Handle Anchors and/or Shoulder Strap Anchors

The process to make handle anchors is rather simple. If you are confused about anything written, it would be a good idea to look at the pictures closely—they ought to be much more descriptive. First, remove the flag part of the marker flag. You will be left with a bit of wire. From one end, measure roughly 0.25" and bend it to 90 degrees, using pliers. From the first bend, measure roughly 0.5" and bend it at the mark another 90 degrees. Slide a tension pin onto the wire. The next bend will be on the other side of the tension pin from the second bend. Make sure there is a small gap for the pin to roll freely. Bend another 90 degrees. Measure another rough 0.5" from the third bend and bend it another 90 degrees. There will be a lot of extra wire, so from the last bend, measure about 0.5" and cut. There should be about a 0.25" gap between the cut and the end where you began. Slide another tension pin on the 0.5" end and pull the second bend so that the 0.25" end is above the open end of the tension pin, then push the end into the tension pin. Using pliers, grasp opposite corners and compress into a trapezoid shape. Grasp the other opposite corners and compress back into a rectangle. All angles should be about 90 degrees.

Notes: You will need two of these anchors for the handle. The process for the shoulder strap anchors is mostly the same, but the tension pins are 2" instead of 1". You will need two shoulder strap anchors as well. If you're not going to make the buckle, you can skip the next step.

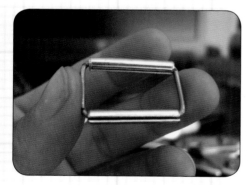

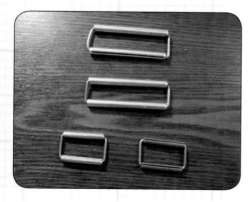

Step 14: Make the Buckle

The process for making the buckle is almost the same as the previous step. There are one or two differences, though. The buckle requires 5/16" × 0.5" tension pins. I had to order these from McMaster-Carr because I wasn't able to find them locally. If you can't find them and don't want to order them specially, you can use a salvaged buckle or some Velcro. The first picture shows the layout of the buckle, minus the clasping pins (I'll wager that there's a trade name for those that I know nothing about). To make the clasping pins, measure about 0.25" from one end of a wire and bend 90 degrees. Measure another 0.25" and bend 90 degrees. The result should be a hook shape. With pliers, close the hook to form a partial loop. There should be enough room inside the loop to fit another wire into it. Trim so the total length is about 2". They are easier to handle this way, and you will end up trimming it to fit soon. Make another, as you need two. To start the buckle loop, measure 0.75" from one end of a wire and bend 90 degrees. Measure 0.5" from the first bend, and bend. Slide two 1" tension pins or one 2" tension pin onto the second bend. Add roughly 0.1" (the width of two marker flag wires) on the other side of the pins and bend. From the third bend, measure around 0.5" and bend. Trim the excess past 0.75" from the last bend. On one side, slide a 0.5" tension pin onto the buckle loop, followed by a clasp pin. Do the same on the other side, making sure the clasping pins are oriented in the same direction. Holding the parts in place, insert the 1" tension pin in the center and compress it closed with the pliers. Consider where the clasping pins lie on the tension pins carefully. Mark just above this point on the clasp pins. Make another mark 0.25" above the previous. Bend at the lower mark slightly downward and trim at the second mark. You can file down any points on the clasp pins now if you want or need to do so. All of the hardware should be completed at this point. We will begin installing them in the next step!

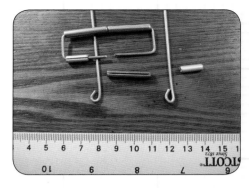

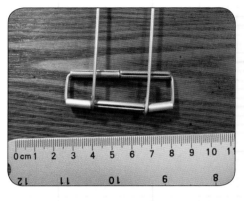

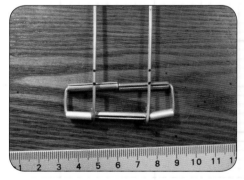

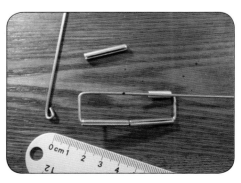

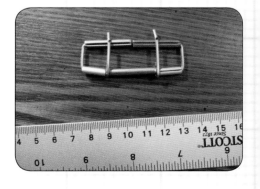

Step 15: Make the Handle

As with all the hardware, if you have something to use instead, go ahead and use it. If you want to make it out of duct tape, good! I have a simple method to make one. Start by folding 12" of duct tape in half lengthwise. Cut another 12" length of duct tape. Place the folded piece of duct tape such that about 1" of it is covering the top half of the unfolded tape. There should be 10" or so of completely exposed tape remaining. Fold the second piece of tape in half lengthwise, which will cover the previous piece and create a 23" strap of duct tape 0.94" wide. Repeat this process until you reach about 5 ft of strap. Coil the strap tightly so that it forms a flat handle. It should be as wide as your palm, at least. Slide the anchors in and position on either side. Count how many loops were made and place the anchors finally in the middle loop. Compress and tape closed with three pieces of tape about 2" long. You are done with the handle, but it needs anchor straps. To make the anchor straps, fold another segment of tape about 12" long in half. Cut another piece about the same length and place the previous piece on the top half of the tape. Fold over. Two of these 12" long, 0.94" wide straps will need to be made. String these pieces into the handle and fold at the halfway point. With handle and anchors made, they can be installed . . . which is in the next step.

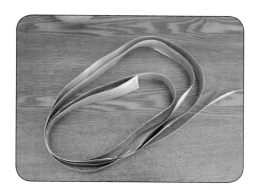

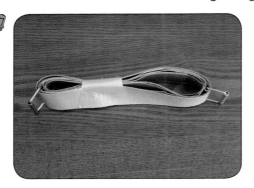

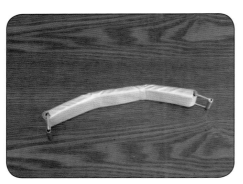

Step 16: Install the Handle

In order to install the handle securely, you must cut slits into the top panel of the bag. It may be difficult to see on the first picture, but I marked the places where slits need to be cut. They can be found easily due to the structure of the bag. Note that the top panel is two segments of tape deep? The center should be easily found. On either side, count 1.5 widths of tape and mark the point at the center. From this point, measure 0.5" above and below the two points. The line between these two points must be cut. After cutting these points, cut 1" segments of tape and cover the seams. Slide the handle anchor straps into these slits. Turn the bag over and get the sacrificial ruler. It is too long and has to be trimmed, in this case. Mark the area to trim, and trim the ruler. This part is important—see for clarification. Place a segment of tape on an anchor strap that is in the center of the bag, centering the ruler over it, and tape them together. Using another piece of tape, tape the other inside anchor strap to the ruler. Now do likewise to the outside anchor straps until the lengths are covered in tape. Entomb the strap/ruler assembly onto the top panel. Remember: You cannot use too much tape. Try to avoid getting tape on the places that are supposed to bend, though. You now have a mostly functional handle that should be reasonably reliable and work well if executed properly. With handle and anchors now handily anchored, you can proceed to install the shoulder strap anchors in the next step.

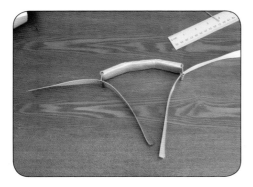

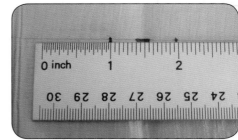

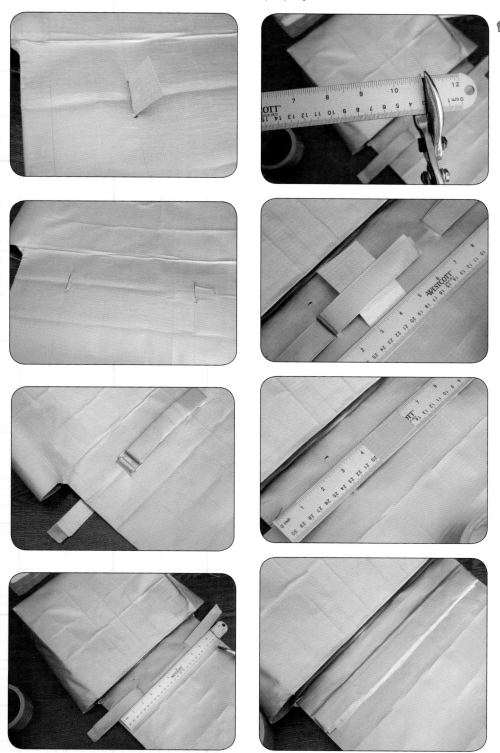

Step 17: Install Shoulder Strap Anchors

Of course, if you don't want to have shoulder straps, you don't have to do this step. If you don't add straps, you really should reinforce the sides. If you want to follow this guide, though, we start by making two short straps. You will employ a similar technique for the buckle straps and full shoulder strap. First, cut two pieces of tape at least 10" long. Try to get them close in length, but overall length isn't very important. Combine both pieces by mating both sticky sides together. Cut two more pieces of similar length and cover the seams. We accomplish this by taking one piece of tape and covering it halfway with the piece previously combined. Fold the piece of tape over to cover the seam, as shown in the picture, albeit not very well. Repeat with another piece on the other side. You should have a strap of tape about 10" long and four pieces of tape thick. Slide the shoulder strap anchor to the center and fold it in half. Cut two pieces of tape roughly 0.5" and secure the strap and anchor in position. Place the anchor and strap on the bag by straddling the strap over one of the sides. Center the strap, then tape it to the bag. Remember when I said that amount of tape and lengths are less important now? I was serious.

You cannot use too much. You can easily use too little, though. The more surface area of duct tape that anchors the shoulder strap to the bag, the more reliable it will be. I cut four roughly 9" pieces of tape and placed two on the outside and two on the inside of the bag. Then I cut a piece about 20" long and threaded through the strap anchor so that half would be laid outside the bag and half on the inside. I did this twice. Not only does it help secure the anchor, but it reinforces the side and makes it more rigid. Repeat this step for the other side and you have two shoulder strap anchors ready to receive a shoulder strap. Next we will install the buckle and have a functional bag!

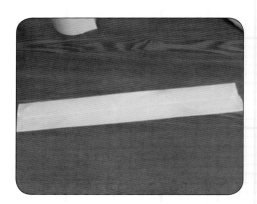

should go towards the bottom panel. Close the flap so it is in a fully closed position. The very top of the tension pins should touch the brim of the flap. Poke holes in the washer strap where the washers are and combine with the buckle. Ensure that the front flap is fully closed and that the buckle is where it should be when you pull on the strap. Pull taught and tape down, trimming any excess. With the strap and buckle in their final positions, tape them down permanently. As before, there is no such thing as using too much tape. Optional: You can make a loop of tape to hold the buckle down. I won't explain how, as it should be obvious with the pictures included. You can also finish the buckle holes any way you prefer. Previously, I used needle/thread, but I don't like the look very much. You should have, at this point, a fully functional bag. You can make a shoulder strap if you have enough spare tape.

Step 18: Install the Buckle

You can easily skip this step and use hook and loop fasteners (Velcro) if you want. You probably determined that before making the buckle, I'm sure. If you want a bag that you made (almost) completely by yourself, continue on. To start off, we need two straps. One will hold the buckle to the bag and the other will hold the washers. Cut an 18" segment of tape and center the buckle onto it about 4" away from one end. Place the washers where the clasp pins lie. Remove the buckle and place another segment of tape similar in length to your first piece. Finish by covering the seams as explained in the previous step. Make another strap, without washers and about 8" long. Again, this was detailed in the previous step. Fold this piece in half and mark the halfway point, if not obvious. Lay the buckle on the strap at the halfway mark and mark where the clasp pins lie. At the holes, cut roughly 0.25" on either side of the half mark. It should be at least as wide as the marker flag wire. Thread the buckle into the strap, so that the pins go through the holes properly. Secure in place with two 0.5" pieces of tape just below the buckle. Place the bag on its back and rough the buckle in. One side of the buckle strap should go up the front panel, while the other

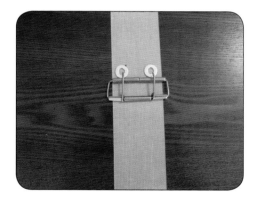

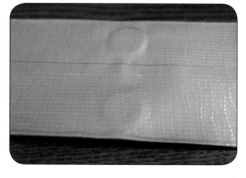

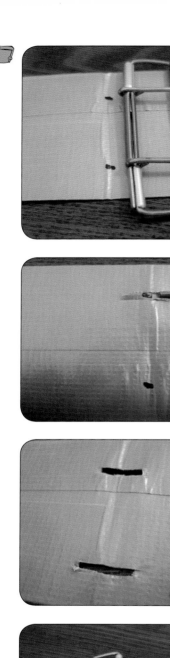

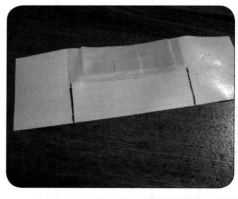

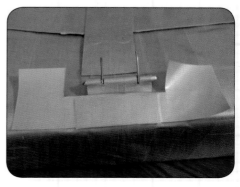

to secure the loop. Push in the other side. Instead of finishing, try the bag on for size. Depending on where you think it is comfortable, adjust the strap. Once you find the perfect length, finish that side. You now have a functional messenger bag!

Step 19: Make and Install Shoulder Strap

If you have strap that you've had in mind to use, you can skip this step. It is easy, though, to make a shoulder strap if you have some extra duct tape. This one is not easily adjusted, unfortunately. In fact, it's very basic, but it gets the job done. I left making it more useful as an exercise for the maker. As with the shoulder strap and buckle straps, this will take the full width of duct tape. Begin by cutting two 1 ft lengths of tape. Rather than placing them directly on top of one another, place them 6" offset, so that there is 6" of exposed tape on either side of the proto-strap. Cut another 1 ft length of tape and cover the exposed sticky side with 6" of the new strip of tape. Continue this process until you reach your desired length. You will probably need between 4 and 6 ft depending on torso size and positioning. For this bag, I made about 5.5 ft, which was about 1 ft too long. Cover the seams, if desired, by cutting lengths of tape and attaching them by aligning the center line of one strap to the side of the other. Fold over. Cut a 12" segment of tape. Cover one end of the strap with 6" of tape and thread through one of the anchors. Push in the strap, making sure the piece of tape is centered. Install the strap by laying the tape cleanly and using another piece of tape perpendicular

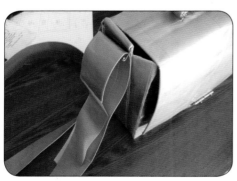

Tool Tote

By fallental
(http://www.instructables.com/
id/Duct-Tape-Tool-Tote/)

This Instructable will show how to make a versatile and *tough* tool tote out of items around the house. This was inspired by an AWP tool bag that I purchased last year and some Craftsman tool bags that I have seen at hardware stores. Enjoy!

Step 1: Materials Needed!

For this project you will only need a few items, and it shouldn't cost much at all. I made mine with everything I had at home.

Materials needed
- Cardboard (and some paperboard for the pockets)
- Scissors (optional)
- Box cutter or razor blade
- A LOT OF DUCT TAPE!

- Tape measure or ruler
- Tools to fill it with

I created this using what I had on hand and it is very handy!

Step 2: Preparation

Before we start taping, some cutting needs to be done.

Using cardboard, a ruler, and a box cutter, cut out three 12" × 8" cardboard pieces and two 8" × 8" cardboard pieces. These will assemble to create the basic structure of your tool tote.

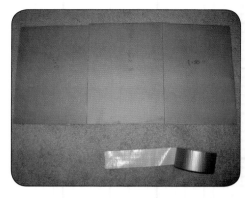

Step 3: Taping the Structure

Lay the three 12" × 8" slats together, with the 12" sides touching. Tape these sides together; the middle slat will be your bottom. Add the 8" × 8" sides and tape them together. Once there is a nice layer of tape, flip the cardboard over and tape the other side.

Step 4: Make the Ends Flexible

Take the ends of the tool bag structure (8″ × 8″ sides) and work them with your hands to make them flexible. Make sure that they will be concave (hollowed inwards) and will face inwards towards the tool bag, which will allow the tool bag to close fully.

Step 5: Tape the Sides Together

Take each adjacent side of board and tape them together, making sure the ends that you just bent curve *inwards*. Once you see the structure taped, tape the inside seems together as well.

Step 6: Creating Handles

Cut out two cardboard handles for your tool bag. Each handle should be roughly 1″ × 7″. Once the handles are cut out, wrap them in duct tape to give them a nice duct tape layer.

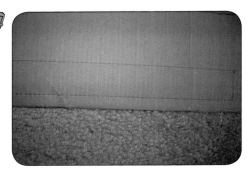

Step 8: Making and Adding End Pockets

These are the pockets that will hold tools and go on the ends of the tool tote (the ends are the cardboard pieces you bent). Start by cutting out two 4″ × 5″ sections of paperboard (to allow flexibility). Once the sections are cut, tape the pockets to the ends of the tool tote (making sure not to tape down the pocket opening).

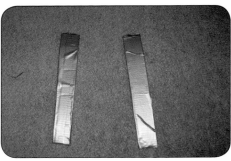

Step 7: Attaching the Handles

To attach the handles, use 5″ strips of duct tape on both sides (eight strips total, four strips per side). Keep 1″ of space between the handle and the tote, and make sure the handles are centered!

Step 9: Making and Adding Side Pockets

These are the pockets that are attached to the side of the tool tote and hold more tools.

Cut out eight 3" × 4" paperboard sections. Four sections will be taped on each side. Now tape each pocket to the side, being cautious not to close the pocket opening. You must tape the pockets individually so that they will be separate pockets instead of one big side pocket (unless of course you want it that way!) Repeat for the opposite side.

Step 10: Add Tools and Bask in Your Glory

Great as a gift for the handy man in the family! Take it anywhere you need basic tools and a water resistant bag for all your works needs.

And it's . . . DUCT TAPE TOUGH!

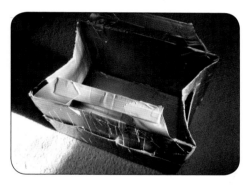

Dog Panniers
By killyourself
(http://www.instructables.com/
id/Duct-Tape-Dog-Panniers/)

Tired of carrying around baggies for poop, baggies of poop, leashes, or food? Make some of these snazzy Duct Tape Dog Panniers, and have your four-legged friend carry their own things. And if you're really lazy, you can throw a bunch of your junk in there too. Keys, cell phone, peanut butter sandwich, rocks, whatever you want.

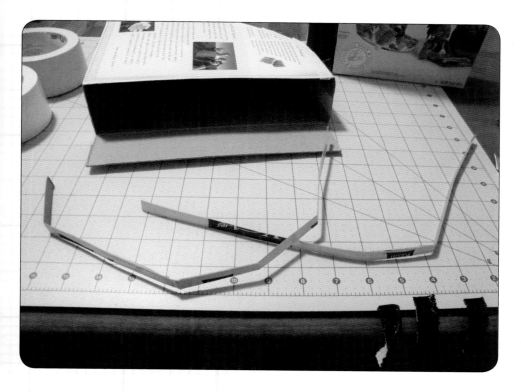

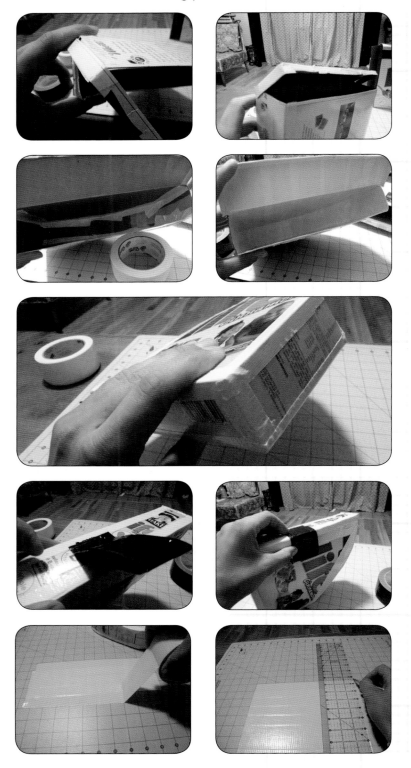

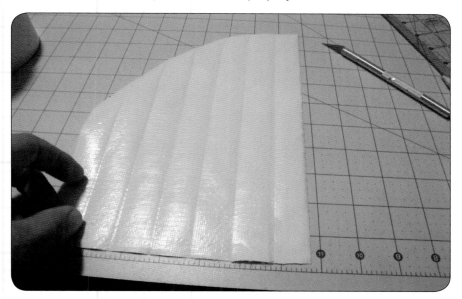

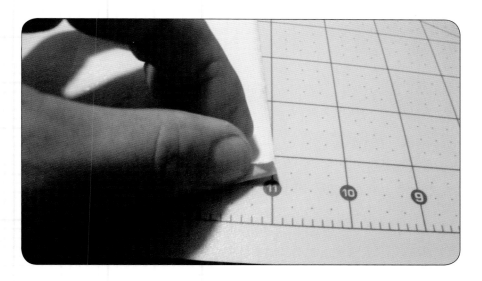

31

Woven Tote

By doormatyay
(http://www.instructables.com/
id/Woven-Duct-Tape-Tote/)

This is just a simple way to make a cute duct tape tote! One of the most important things about making anything with duct tape is to use good quality duct tape. I recommend Duck brand duct tape, but if you find something just as good or better, use that! If you haven't worked with duct tape like this before, it might be a little challenging, but the only setback is that it might take you a little longer. You will need three differently colored rolls of duct tape, scissors, and a ruler (in inches). In this tutorial, I labeled the duct tapes for ease of description: A is the purple; B is the peace sign/blue; C is the green.

Step 1: Cut A Strips

With color A, cut ten strips of tape 9" long each.

Step 2: Fold A Strips

Fold A strips in half horizontally

Step 3: Cut and Fold B Strips

With color B, cut 18 strips of tape 6" long each. Fold these in half horizontally as well.

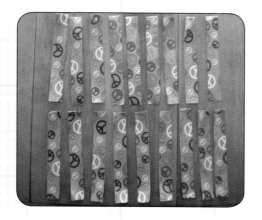

Step 4: Lay Out A Strips

With color C, cut two strips 6.5" long each. Lay color C strips down on the table sticky side up. Have them parallel to each other and about 9" apart. Lay five A strips perpendicular to B strips, overlapping about 1/4" on each side, leaving about 1" of color C on each side. If any of your strips have imperfections on them, make sure they are facing up; then they will be on the inside of the bag. Smooth out the strips to make sure they are all lying straight and even.

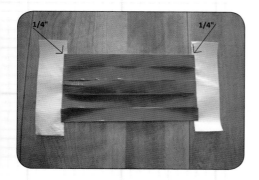

Step 5: Weave in B Strips

Weave nine B strips into A strips. Be careful not to accidentally un-stick

A strips from C strips while weaving. Make sure they are all fairly tight together. (This part is a little tricky). Try to push them towards each other to ensure tightness, but do not overlap B strips with other B strips.

Step 6: Fold Over Sides

Fold the C strips over the woven pattern. Be careful to not trap air in the fold. Cut off excess C tape and turn the strips over. This will be one of the sides.

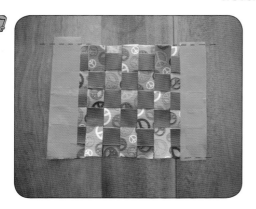

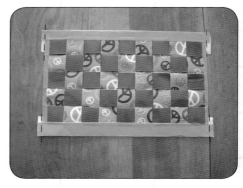

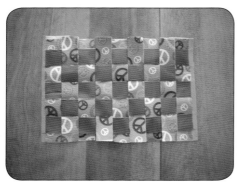

Step 8: Create Second Side

Repeat steps 4–8 with remaining strips. You should have two complete woven sides.

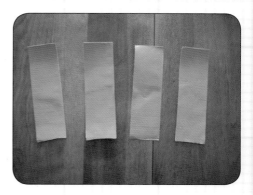

Step 7: Finish Off the Sides

Cut two strips of C tape 9.5" each. Overlap one C strip over the front of the woven pattern on a side that doesn't already have C tape. Fold C strip over onto the other side (the inside). Repeat with other side. Cut off excess tape.

Step 9: Create Solid Sides

Cut four strips of C 12.5" each. Fold them in half vertically. Tape two of the strips together by the long sides. Do the same with the other two. Cut the end sides to match the length of the woven sides.

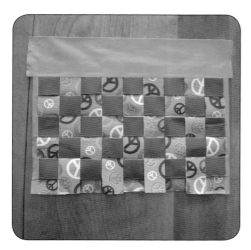

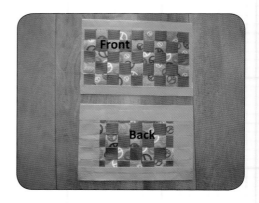

Step 10: Attach Solid Sides

Tape the solid sides to one of the woven sides from the front, using pieces of C tape that are the length of the woven side. For extra stability, tape from the inside as well.

Step 11: Create Solid Bottom

Cut two strips of C 18.5" each. Fold in half vertically. Tape the two pieces together by the long sides. Cut to fit the length of the woven sides.

Step 12: Attach Solid Bottom

Tape the bottom to the woven piece with the solid sides on it already. For extra stability, add tape from the inside, too.

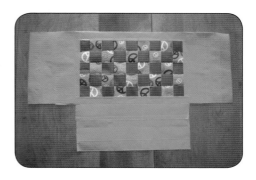

Step 13: Begin Assembling Body of Tote

Tape the bottom end of the solid sides to the sides of the bottom piece. This can get tricky. For extra stability, tape from both the outside and inside of the seams.

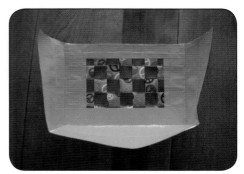

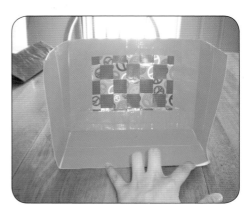

Step 14: Finishing Body of Tote

Tape the other woven side to the two solid ends and to the bottom piece. This is much harder than it sounds and may take you a couple of tries to get it just right! Again, use tape from both sides for more stability.

Step 15: Create Handles

Choose either tape A or B and cut two strips 14" each. Fold in half horizontally. Tape the strips to the inside of the bag with small pieces of color C tape. Finished! Enjoy your new, do-it-yourself tote bag!

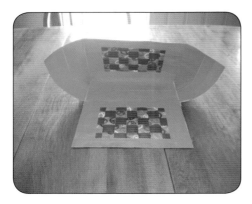

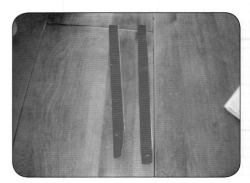

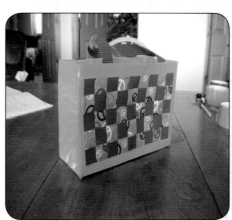

This is my newest creation, a 15" × 15" × 4" woven duct tape tote/purse. It's super sturdy and quite impressive!

Step 1: Items Needed

- Approximately 120 yd of duct tape (I used three different colors with two rolls being 60 yd each of black)
- A scissors
- A razor blade
- Ruler/tape measure
- Cardboard
- Pen/pencil/marker
- 550 cord/paracord (parachute cord)
- (Magnets optional)

Step 2: Tape Sheets

1. Using the color tape that you have the most of (mine was black), cut a strip of tape 15.5". Lay the first one down glue side up. Carefully line up the second strip over the first (glue side to glue side) overlapping the widths half way. Fold over the second half of the exposed glue-side-up strip to make a clean edge.
2. Flip the combined strips over, leaving glue side up. Lay the next layer down, overlapping tape layers about 0.25" to 0.5".
3. Repeat step 2 until the sheet of tape is 15" exactly.

   Note: Using a ruler (mine was 16" long), I measured a straight line on the table to align my final strip of tape so it would be straight and measured the sheet so it would line up with the line I drew exactly 15" away.
4. Using your ruler and the razor, cut a straight edge on the uneven edges, leaving a clean line. Repeat on the other side and measure to make sure it's 15" wide. You should now have a solid sheet of duct tape that is exactly 15" × 15".

   Note: Cut as close to the first uneven edge as possible, without leaving a jagged edge of tape. This should leave enough room on the other side to play with to make a clean cut.
5. Repeat steps 1–4 again leaving you with two 15" × 15" sheets.
6. Repeat steps 1–4 again, but this time make two sheets that are 4" × 15".

   Note: Set these sheets aside for later use.

(I have six 15.25" strips of black, twelve 15.25" strips of orange, and thirty 15.25" strips of white for this pattern.

Note: The strips are all slightly longer than they need to be to accommodate the shortening of the strips through the weaving process to come.

Step 3: Woven Strips

The following steps will need to be repeated a *lot*! You've been warned.

1. Your will need to cut a strip of tape that is 38".
2. Fold the tape lengthwise into approximate thirds (about 5/8" folded over).
3. Fold the tape over again, making one strip.
4. Repeat steps 1–3 until you have 20 strips total of the 38" strips—yes, 20 total.
5. Repeat steps 1–3 again, making two strips totaling 5 ft (60") long. These will be your handles for the bag.
6. Depending on the pattern you have planned on, you'll need to repeat steps 1–3 again until you have 48 strips total, all 15.25" long.

Step 4: Purse Bottom

First, get your cardboard; the stiffer the better!

1. Cut out two rectangles measuring 15" × 4", with the corrugation running lengthwise.
2. Cut out a rectangle measuring 15" × 4", with the corrugation running widthwise.
3. Stack the layers together so the corrugation is alternating, with the widthwise corrugation in the middle.
4. Cover the entire stack in tape, making a solid plank. Make sure to cover all the edges.

Step 5: Assembly of the Inner Bag

For my design, I covered the top of the cardboard plank in white to make it easy to see into the bottom of the bag. That will come later.

Grab the two 15" × 15" sheets and the two 15" × 4" sheets.

1. We'll work with the 4" wide sheet first. With the strips of the sheets running vertically (the cut edges on top and bottom), align the bottom edge to the bottom edge of the plank. Using a 4" strip of tape, lay it over the bottom edge of the sheet half way and fold the rest over the underside of the plank.
2. With the sheet standing up (or hanging down depending how you look at it) apply another 4" strip to the inside edge.

3. Repeat steps 1 and 2 for the remaining three sides. (This is when I applied the white tape to the plank)

Note: Now comes a little bit of a tricky part. A second pair of helping hands may be beneficial.

4. Using a 15" strip of tape, tape up the seam of the two sheets on the outer edge. Keep the edges tightly together.
5. Using a 15" strip of tape, tape up the seam of the two sheets on the inner edge. Get the tape as far into the crease as you can (bend it flat if you can). You should notice about 0.5" of tape overhanging the top of the sheet. Trim it off flush with the sheet.
6. Repeat steps 4 and 5 with the other three seams. Keep in mind that the closer you get to the final seam, the harder it will be to get the inside seam flat. (This is where an extra set of hands comes in handy to help apply the tape).

Note: Once the bag is finished, set it aside for later.

Step 6: Assembly of the Woven Sheet

Prepare to spend a lot of time taping and weaving!

Grab yourself a 15.5" strip and a 36" strip. Throughout the rest of this stage and pretty much the rest of the Instructable, you will be using literally 1,000+ pieces of tape that are about 1" × 0.5"! (Let's call these small pieces of tape tacks.)

Note: It is important that you make sure, from here on out, all the strips of tape have the exposed folded edge all facing the same side! This will make a cleaner looking finished product. Also, I will be describing in generality for the pattern. But if you care to repeat it, possibly with different colors, the pattern will go (lengthwise from top to bottom) six white, three orange, six white, three orange, three white, six black, three white, three orange, six white, three orange, six white.

1. At the end of the 36" strip, tape half of the tack to it. Align the long strip perpendicular to the 15.25" strip. Fold the other half of the tack underneath the 15.25" strip.
2. Repeat step 1 directly next to the first 36" strip, making sure that the long strips are touching edge to edge. But this time put the long strip under the 15.25" strip and fold the tack over instead of under.
3. Repeat steps 1 and 2 until you have the first seven columns of 36" strips taped.
4. For the eighth column of long strips, grab one of the two 60" long strips. Measure 17.25" from the tape end down on the seventh column strip and note where the mark is. This is where the end of the 60" strip should start. Following the over-under pattern, tack the eighth column to the 15.25" strip and gently lay the excess strip to the side.

5. Using the 36" strips again, repeat steps 1 and 2 again until you have six more columns applied.

6. For the 15th column, grab the other end of the 60" strip and measure out 17.25" like you did in step 4. Tack the handle in place (still using the over-under weaving pattern).

Note: Make sure the strip isn't twisted up and that the folded exposed edge of the strip curves around so that it's the underside of the strap.

7. Using the 36" strips again, repeat steps 1 and 2 again until you have seven more columns applied. This should bring you to the end of the 15.25" strip. Tack the ends down, and, if a slight bit of strip overhangs past the last 36" strip, trim it off (it's why we made it a touch longer).

8. Grab your next 15.25" strip, and as stated . . . start weaving, over and under opposite to the previous row. I find it easier to tuck the row under one column at a time.

Note: Make sure you pull the rows together as tight as you can without bending or creasing the two of them *while simultaneously* keeping the columns straight and as tight together as you can without bending or creasing them. A nice tight weave!

9. Repeat step 8 for the next eight rows, making nine in total.

10. Set it aside for a bit. Now we're going to get a little more creative!

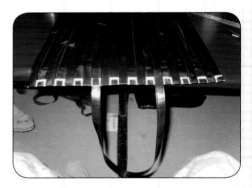

Step 7: Assembly of the Woven Pockets

We'll be weaving pockets in the same manner as the outer woven sheet.

1. We need to cut eight strips at 8.75". (For my design, these are the six white and two orange horizontal strips.)
2. Next we need to cut ten strips at 7" (the black vertical strips).
3. Fold the strips into thirds again like back in step 3 (the 36", 60", and 15.25" strips).
4. Grab your first horizontal strip (orange). Fold it in half and note where the center mark is. In the over-under styling of the previous step, tack the ten vertical strips (black) to the first horizontal strip.

   Note: Keep in mind that you need to keep the strips perpendicular to each other.
5. Grab the next horizontal 8.75" strip. Keeping the ends lined up, weave the strips together, tacking the new row to the previous row as in Step 6: Assembly of the Woven Sheet.
6. Repeat step 5 until all eight rows are woven together.
7. Cut a strip of tape to go edge to edge from the first to last vertical strip. Lay the edge of the tape directly over the first row, sealing the woven strips together. Fold the rest of the tape over to the back side. Press firmly.

8. With the finished pocket, flip the whole thing over. Cut strips long enough to go edge to edge from the first to last vertical strips.
9. Now, overlay these cut strips over the back of the pocket, covering all the tacks. Each layer of these strips will overlap about 0.5". This will give it a clean and finished look, especially when you open the pocket.

   Set this woven pocket to the side for a few minutes; we'll get back to it shortly.

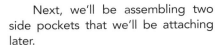

Next, we'll be assembling two side pockets that we'll be attaching later.

10. You'll need to cut strips out at the following lengths: six horizontal strips 6" long and seven vertical strips 5" long.

11. Repeat step 3 for all the strips you just cut.

12. This time when you fold the first row in half, note where the center mark is. This is where the center of the seven vertical strips will be placed for proper spacing.

13. Repeat steps 5–9 until you have finished the side pocket.

14. Trim all the loose ends flush and make them the length of one vertical row past the first and last vertical row.

15. Repeat steps 10–14 again to make a second pocket.

Set these two smaller pockets aside for now.

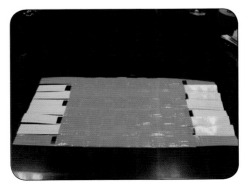

Step 8: Assembly of Woven Sheet Continued

Alright now comes the fun part—attaching the front pocket to the woven sheet.

Now that the front pocket is pre-made and we have our woven sheet with the first nine rows woven, it's time to combine the two into one.

1. Take your pocket and lay it over the woven sheet. In my pattern, you'll notice the pocket will span from the last orange strip across the six white strips and end on the first orange strip of the three in the pattern. You'll also notice that the spacing of the handles is eight columns from handle strip to handle strip, while the pocket you made spans ten columns.

2. You'll need four strips measuring 5/8" × 2", plus one tack strip per row for all the rows of the pocket to adhere it.

3. With your pocket lying over the woven sheet, locate where the last column is and move one more to the right. You'll see where the loose end of the first row lays over the last row of the sheet. Tuck the 2" long strip behind the last row of the sheet, making sure the edge of the strip is flush with the bottom edge of the row. This will help conceal any unsightly seam lines. Wrap the 2" strip over the top of the pocket's first-row loose end and tuck

it under the back side of the last roof of the sheet.

4. Weave the rest of this loose end under the next column and over the following one. Repeat the tucking of the 2" strip behind the back row, over the pocket row, and underneath the back row again. There should be just enough loose end left that you can lay it under the following column. It'll be covered when you continue the weaving process.

5. Repeat steps 3 and 4 for the left side of the pocket on the first row. The only difference is with the weave: when you weave the loose end under the third column, snip off any excess and just tack the loose end under the column.

   Note: Any time the loose ends go over a column when weaving, you'll use the 2" strip to hold it, and any time it ends under the column, you just need to use a tack.

   Now that the top row of the pocket is woven into the sheet, we need to continue not only the pockets but the rest of the sheet.

6. Flip the sheet with the now-attached pocket upside down. Grab your next 15.25" strip and weave/tack it into place on the woven sheet as you did for the first nine rows. (In my pattern, the next color was white, which matches the next row of the pocket). Once finished, flip the entire thing over again.

7. Repeat steps 3–5 with the second row of the pocket. Keep in mind to follow the pattern of the weave. It will be opposite of the previous row. Use the three 5/8" × 2" strips and the one tack on this second row to adhere this row of the pocket.

8. Continue to do steps 6 and 7 for the rest of rows of the pocket.

9. With the pocket now fully attached/woven in, we can continue with the simpler process of weaving just the sheet. Continue your pattern in guidance with steps from Step 6: Assembly of the Woven Sheet.

10. When you finally reach the halfway mark, you'll see you have come to the end of the handle strips. Take the second 60" strip and tape the ends of the strips to one another. Continue the weaving process.

11. With all of the rows finally finished, you should have some loose ends hanging out at the ends of the 36" strips. Trim these ends flush with the final row of the sheet and tack all of the ends to the final row.

    Now that all of the loose ends are trimmed and tacked in place, it's time to finish off the sheet.

12. Like when making the pockets, we're going to seal up the backside. You'll need to cut strips 15" long and line the back of the sheet, covering all the tack strips. Overlay each strip about 0.5".

13. Just like the top edges of the pockets, we need to lay tape the exact length and width of the sheet over the outer rows and columns, and fold it over to the back side. Now you have a finished woven sheet with all edges sealed up. For the edges with the handles, you'll need to make a few cuts so you can wrap the tape around the handle. I cut a slit at the very base of the handle (in the tape to be folded over) matching the width of the handle. Then, on the inner edge of the handle, I cut at 90 degrees from the slit I had just made to the edge of the tape to be wrapped over. This will allow the tape to wrap over and around the handle and will seal everything up nicely.

    To strengthen the handle straps, I went with 10 ft of 550 cord/paracord/parachute cord. The sheath has a breaking point of about 305 lbs. I fully understand

that this may seem like a slight overkill for the weight ratio, but it's easily flattened and certainly strong enough. The inner strands hold about 35 pounds a strand, but I didn't want the thin strands potentially cutting their way through the tape of the straps over time.

14. Remove all the inner strands from the outer sheath.

15. Laying the sheath approximately 1/4 of the way down the length of the woven sheet (in line with the handle straps), tape the sheath to the back edge of the woven sheet.

This next step is a little troublesome.

16. Cut a strip of tape about 25" long. Lining up the end of the tape to the edge of the sheet, tape the strip along the entire length of the handle. Center the strap in the middle of the tape strip even while it curves around the handle.

Note: Be careful not to let the tape fold in on itself and get stuck to anything else.

17. Lay the sheath on the underside of the handle strap, and carefully fold over one edge of the tape over the sheath and the other side. *Press firmly* on the seam you just created.

18. Route the sheath across the length of the woven sheet and repeat steps 16 and 17 again.

19. You'll have several inches of rope overlapping each other. Tape the rope down and press firmly all along the seams.

For the purpose of my pattern, I later added a 5/8" × ~25" strip of orange to the underside of the handle straps. It gave it accent coloring, and it covered up and helped seal the seams of tape holding in the rope.

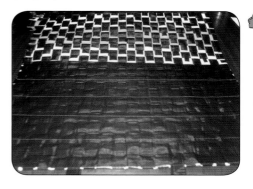

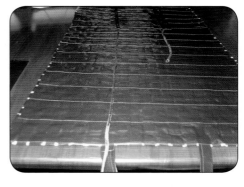

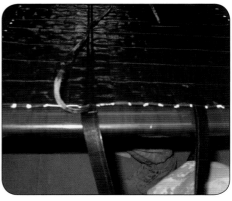

Step 9: Assembly of the Side Pockets

Now we will attach the side pockets to the inner bag.

The first thing you may notice is that the side pockets are just a tad wider than the width of the 4" inner bag we made back in Step 1: Assembly of the Inner Bag. This is fine; if we made it just 4", the pocket would be too tight to use it for anything useful. This will give it a slight bowing out. The front pocket didn't need because since the sidewall is flexible.

Before I got started with this step, I covered both 4" wide side walls of the bag in orange.

1. Grab the two side pockets you created earlier and the inner bag.
2. Cut two strips of tape four to 4.5" long. Align one strip to each side of the pocket. It should completely cover the loose ends (the black strips, not the orange ones.)
3. Align the one edge of the outer vertical strip to the edge of the bag. (Make sure the edge of the bottom of the last horizontal row is flush with the bottom edge of the bag.) Tape the pocket to the back with the already attached to the pocket.

4. Wrap the pocket around to the other edge of the 4" wall and tape it down in the same manner.
5. Cut yourself seven strips of 0.5" × 2" tape. Starting with the center vertical row loose end, tack the loose end down to the underside of the bag. Do so with the other loose ends, working from the center outwards.

   Note: To make it look better, as I moved outwards taping the loose ends down, I taped them on an increasing angle to help keep the bowing shape of the pocket.
6. To help seal it all in place, cut a strip of tape about 13" long and wrap it from one sidewall, down underneath (over the 2" long tacks), and back up the other side wall. Press firmly.
7. Repeat steps 2–6 for the pocket on the other side of the bag.

of duct tape, I needed something pretty strong. Being resourceful, I dismantled a broken portable hard drive and stripped it of the two rare earth magnets that were inside—just the perfect strength and size for what I needed. I simply taped them on the outside of the inner bag with a square of tape. And they won't be visible when the woven sheet is fixed to the inner bag.

Depending on how well and straight you wove the outer sheet will affect how easy it will be to put the two pieces together. I found it easier to lay the top edge of the inner bag to the top edge of the woven sheet.

1. Just like back in Step 8: Assembly of the Woven Sheet Continued, cut a strip of tape 15" long and lay it over the end of the sheet (only covering the first woven row). Cut the same notches in the tape as you did before to allow you to wrap the tape over and around the handles. Fold the tape over the sheet and onto the inside of the inner bag.

   Note: To keep it all together a little better, I rolled long strips of tape back over itself like I was making double sided tape. I lay a few across the length of the woven sheet and on the center where the bottom of the plank would sit.

2. Wrap the rest of the woven sheet down and around to the other side of the inner bag and repeat step 1.

3. To seal the four edges of the tote, you'll need four strips of tape 16" long. Trim the strip so they are only 0.75" wide. This will make it only overlap the outer strips of the woven bag and the outer strips of the side pockets, matching the rest of the project.

4. Align the edge of the strip you just made to the outer row of the woven sheet and fold it over the sidewall of the inner bag. (Make sure you cover the outer row of the pouch on the side.) Neatly tuck and fold the excess

Step 10: Finalizing Assembly

As a last minute idea, I decided to put some magnets in this tote bag. Now, since this is pretty thick with layers tape hanging off the bottom edge over and under, making a nice corner.

Note: The tape you just folded over partially covers the opening to the side wall pocket. Carefully make a slit for the pocket opening and lay the rest of the tape flat.

5. Repeat steps 2–5 again for the other three remaining edges.

6. Cut two strips of tape about 0.75" × 4.5" long and repeat step 4 for the bottom edges of the pocket/woven sheet.

7. To finalize the tote, cut two strips of tape at five to 5.5" long. Align the tape to the top edge of the purse where the first strip is and fold it over to the inside of the inner bag.

Congrats! You now have a stylish, hand-woven High Quality Duct Tape Tote Bag!

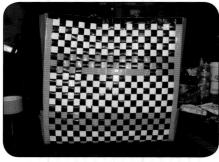

No-Sew Zipper Pouch

By Sarah James
(scoochmaroo)
(http://www.instructables.com/id/No-Sew-Duct-Tape-Zipper-Pouch/)

This project is similar to another one you'll find in the awesome book *Simply Sublime Bags* by Jodi Kahn.

Step 1: Materials

- Paper to make a pattern (optional)
- Fabric— about 8" × 11" or so (since I used US legal paper). Customize to suit your needs.
- Seven-inch zipper
- Duct tape in a color of your choice
- Stapler and staples
- Scissors
- Pen

Take your duct tape skills to the next level with this great zippered pouch. The interior is water-proof, making this bag great for carrying, pens, make-up, whatever you can imagine.

Choose an outer fabric that suits your personality and function. I knew when I saw this adorable Hello Kitty satin in my favorite color, I just couldn't resist. In fact, I blame the fabric itself for the inception of this entire project. Sometimes it just calls to you!

Step 2: Make Pattern

Using this simple sheet of paper, I was able to make a quick and accurate pattern. Cut off one margin along the red line. Fold the paper in thirds to simulate where you want the zipper to be. Lay the pattern on top of the fabric and mark a line about 0.5" outside of the edge as your taping area.

Step 3: Tape Fabric

Prepare the back of your fabric with strips of slightly overlapping strips of duct tape. Cut strips of tape to extend slightly beyond marked lines. Overlap rows of tape at small amounts. Re-trace the pattern onto the taped fabric. Trace 0.5" seam allowance around the outside of the perimeter. Cut the fabric along the outer line.

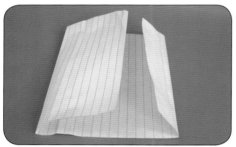

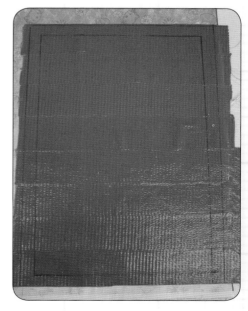

Step 4: Apply Zipper

It's easier than it seems to add a zipper to this simple pouch. Lay the zipper upside down on one of the short edges of your face-up fabric (see picture). Staple it to the fabric next to the zipper teeth, using the seam marked on the taped side as a guide. Fold the fabric in half, lining up the unstapled edge of the zipper with the opposite edge of the fabric. Staple as above.

Step 5: Close Sides

Now we determine once and for all where we want that zipper to line up. Use the paper pattern as your guide for where to fold the fabric. Staple along the sides, using the seam lines as a guide. Open the zipper before completing final edge (so you can turn it right side out when you're done).

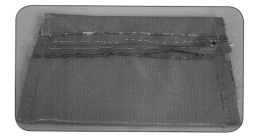

Step 6: Tape Down Raw Edges

All that's left is to tape up the raw edges! Tape over the exposed edges of zipper. Lay tape over the staples on the front side and fold SA to the back. Repeat on other side.

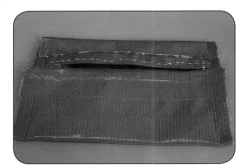

Step 7: Finish!

Turn the pouch right side out and fill it with your stuff! I hope you've enjoyed this simple yet attractive ten-minute project.

Stripy Pencil Case

By nanapoly
(http://www.instructables.com/
id/That-stripey-duct-tape-
pencil-case/)

A practical case to carry a few pens, pencils, mascara perhaps.

You will need

- Cardboard/postcards
- Several rolls of duct tape, for color and variety
- Cutting mat and blade
- Ruler

Step 1: Preparation

Four pieces of cardboard are needed to reinforce the pencil case. The sizes I used are: A) 3.15" × 6.75" (base); B) 3.15" × 4.33" (top flap); C) 3.15" × 4"; D) 3.15" × 0.6". Postcards are lightweight and suitable for this. A cutting board helps to quickly measure the pieces.

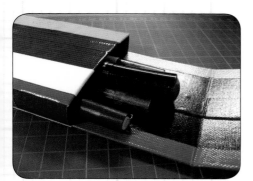

Step 2: Lining the Pieces

Line all the pieces with black duct tape on one side, because it will make the inside of the pencil case look good. The top flap and base should be taped while it's folded, so that later your pencil case will naturally close.

Step 3: Giving It Shape

Attach all the pieces together.

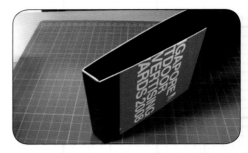

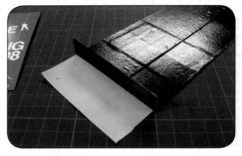

Step 4: Holding It Together

Prepare the duct tape on the cutting mat. Make sure the duct tape strips overlap each other by about 0.5" or more, so that the entire piece can be lifted. Also prepare two strips of duct tape, 0.6" wide. Slowly lift the big piece of duct tape, and place your pencil case on the top 4.3" of it, placed roughly in the middle. Cut the bottom part as shown. Carefully stick the blue strips as shown. Be very careful because when duct tape sticks to duct tape it's really ugly and impossible to remove. Use the blade to trim excess blue tape. Fold the duct tape and paste.

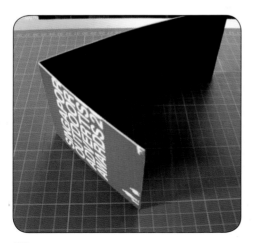

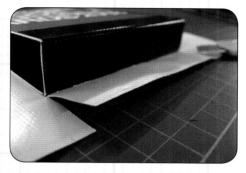

Step 5: Creating the Long Strip

Prepare the main duct tape as shown in the picture. Again, make sure the pieces overlap each other so they can be lifted as one big piece. Paste. Fold in the excess piece tightly. Smooth out creases. With the top flap bent, continue the pasting. This ensures your pencil case has a natural closure.

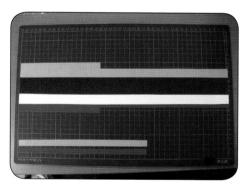

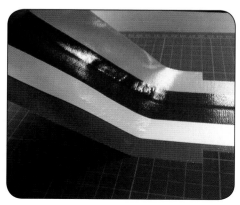

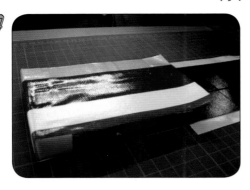

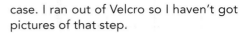
case. I ran out of Velcro so I haven't got pictures of that step.

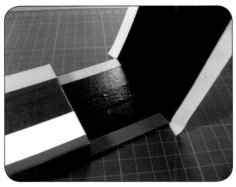

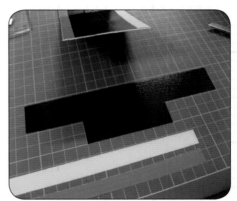

Step 6: Final Trim

Prepare another black duct tape strip as shown. If you have gotten this far, this step is fairly easy. Finally, attach some Velcro for the flap to stick to the

Section 2
Wallets

Quality Wallet with (Optional) Change Pouch

By Phillip Jones (PhilmanJ)
(http://www.instructables.com/
id/Quality-Duct-Tape-Wallet-
with-optional-Change-Po/)

This is another take on the duct tape wallet. As a Canadian, I end up with a lot of coins, so I needed a coin pouch. My build adds a change pouch and tries to use as little tape as possible.

Materials Required

- Duct tape
- Plastic card for sizing
- Scissors
- Razor (cutting board to go with it)

Materials optional

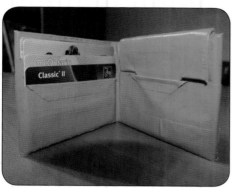

on the inside of the pouch. Place them on the outside, half hanging over, at the halfway mark of the wallet. Fold them in, and fold up the wallet. (Power tip: If you fold the wallet up before folding in the two inner pieces, you can see if they are too far down or up.)

Fold the two pieces that are sticking up down along the edge and trim the ends.

Step 1: Main Money Pouch

The first step is creating the main pouch that will hold your paper money. First you will need four pieces of tape, approximately 8.5". This will be trimmed at the end to around 8". Lay them on top of each other, overlapping about 1/4 inch. You can use the lines in the fabric to help you line up your tape.

Then cut four more pieces of equal length. Lay the first on top, sticky side to sticky side, letting half of the strip go over the edge. Lay the rest down, overlapping the top piece again by about 1/4 inch. The final piece should only cover half of the bottom piece. *Careful* laying the sticky sides together, as it is very hard to separate the tape if you mess up.

Fold the exposed top and bottom pieces over. Now you have your duct tape cloth! Trim both sides to around 8".

Finally, fold the cloth in half. Cut two pieces of tape a little bigger than the height of the wallet. These will be

Step 2: Card Slots

In this step, you will be making the card slots. First, fold down the tape on the left side, as this will be covered up by the pouches. Trim the excess. I like to cut the pieces I need first: Cut three pieces a little longer than twice the length of a credit/debit card (about 7.5inches). Optional: I like the card to stick out a bit more than usual with the standard width of tape. So I trim about 0.25" from the top. Wrap the tape tightly around two cards, sticky side out. Cut three more pieces a little bit longer than a card (3.5"). Cut two pieces the length of the card, and then cut them in half lengthwise, making four pieces the length of a card. Cut the corners of three of these pieces. Finally, cut three pieces about 5.5". Lay the 3.5" tape about halfway down the wallet. Next, lay a roll in the middle of it. Fold half the tape on the bottom of the 3.5" piece up onto the roll, creating the bottom of the pocket. Place two cards in to test the position. Take the one piece without the corners cut and place it over the back line of the pouch. This helps the

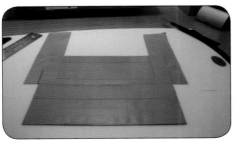

card slide in. Line it up with the top of the wallet. Place a card over the top part of the pouch so your piece does not stick to it when you're placing it. Place a 5.5" piece over the pouch. Make sure it goes past the middle of the wallet and wraps around back. Place it upside down first to find out the position. Line the top of the tape with the top of the pouch. Make the next pouch by sticking the bottom piece (3.5") to the bottom of the loop. Then place it under the first pouch about 0.25" down. Take a piece with the corners cut off and place it over the lip of the top pouch, lining up the middle with the lip. The front part should go into the second pouch. Again this helps the cards go in. Note: The cut corners make it easier to place the tape in the pouch. And make it look cool. Lay another 5.5" piece like the first. Repeat the steps for the second pouch to make the third. If the bottom piece goes over the bottom of the wallet, trim it. Sometimes I had to trim the corners more. Scissors work great at this. Cut a piece a little bigger than the height of the wallet. Place this piece going down the right-half side of the card slots. Finally, cut a piece about 5.5" to wrap around the bottom. Let it go over the left edge and trim with scissors.

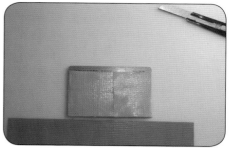

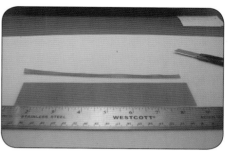

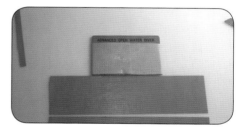

quality wallet with (optional) change pouch

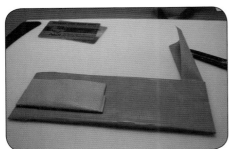

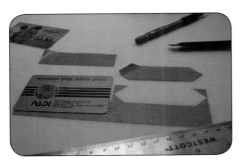

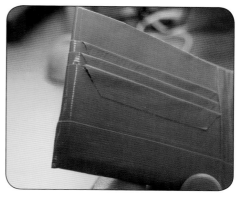

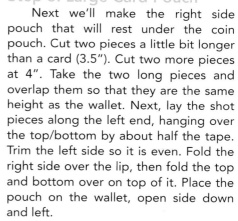

Step 3: Large Card Pouch

Next we'll make the right side pouch that will rest under the coin pouch. Cut two pieces a little bit longer than a card (3.5"). Cut two more pieces at 4". Take the two long pieces and overlap them so that they are the same height as the wallet. Next, lay the shot pieces along the left end, hanging over the top/bottom by about half the tape. Trim the left side so it is even. Fold the right side over the lip, then fold the top and bottom over on top of it. Place the pouch on the wallet, open side down and left.

If at this point, you do not want a change pouch: Cut one piece 4" long, and two to the width of the pouch. Wrap the 4" piece around the front of the pouch and the back of the wallet. Place the two other pieces on the top and bottom of the pouch, wrapping them over to the front of the wallet and inside of the money pouch. Make sure to unstick the inside wrapping piece so you can attach the top of the pouch. Wrap the long piece on the left of the wallet down over the right-hand side of the wallet and trim. Cut a piece the height of the pouch, cut it in half lengthwise, and cut the corners. Use it to wrap the lip of the pouch. You're done!

Otherwise, wrap the right side tape down to secure the pouch in place. Trim the bottom.

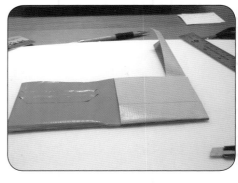

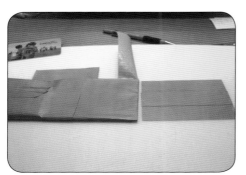

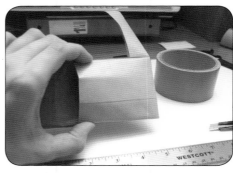

and back cover for the little pouch. Do the same for the width. Cut the corners on these lines. It should resemble a Superman symbol. Place it over the top lip at its widest point and fold over. Tuck the bottom inside the small pouch. (You could do this with two simple pieces, but this looks better.) Cut a 0.5" piece of tape. Cut the corners off and place it on the lip of the small front pouch.

Step 4: Coin Pouch

We will basically be making a big credit card pouch. Cut one piece the length of the right pouch (3.5"). Cut two pieces the length of the wallet (8"). Again, overlap the long pieces to make them the height of the wallet. Make a loop with the long pieces the width of the pouch (wrap around a card). Add the short piece on the bottom of the roll to create the bottom of the change pouch. Place this pouch on top of the other. Start with the right side first to get the placement, as it is easier to remove from the non-sticky side of the tape. Cut two pieces of tape 4.5 inches long (about an inch bigger than the pouch). Place one on the top of the pouch; line up the top of the tape with the top lip. Wrap it inside the pouch and to the outside of the wallet. Cut a piece 4" long. Make a roll the width of the tape (slightly less than 2"). You can also make it roll around a card (short end), but I like it a bit smaller than that to make it the width of the tape. Place this in the center and on the bottom of the pouch. Place the second 4.5" piece on the bottom, line up with the top of the smaller pouch, and wrap it inside the left pouch and to the outside of the wallet. Cut two pieces the length of the pouch (3.5"). Use one of them to cover up the bottom of the pouches. Place the other beside the wallet. Mark with a pencil the lines for the middle and top pouch, allowing a bit to go over the coin pouch lip. This will be our lip cover

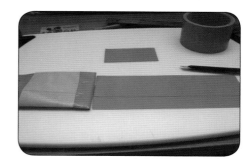

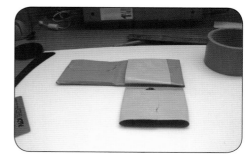

quality wallet with (optional) change pouch

70

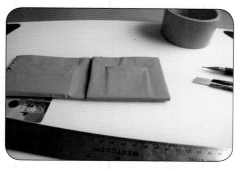

the front pouch and you're done! If you want, you can put some tape over the outside edges to clean up the back, but that is up to you!

Step 5: Coin Pouch Flap

Final Step!

Cut two pieces the width of the pouch (3.5 inches). To ensure the flap comes down enough, place one of these pieces face down in line with the small front pouch. Keeping it in line, wrap it over to the inside of the cash pocket. Then peel it up off the front of the pouch. Place the second piece in line with the top of the flap, and have it go into the coin pouch. Cut about an inch (the height of the flap) of tape and cut it in half. Cut it in half again. Use two of these pieces to close the side of the flap. Cut a piece 2.5". Center it inside the pouch, coming up and over the flap. Fold the end of the tape into a triangle. Cut two more pieces about the length of a card. Place the tape inside the cash part of the wallet flush with the flap. Split the tape where the triangle starts and fold the thinner flap into the pouch. Trim the remaining tape to the height of the triangle. Fold over the triangle. Repeat for the other side. Tuck the triangle into

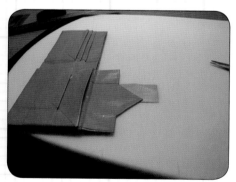

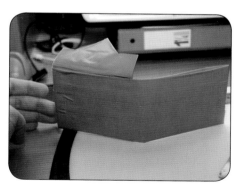

Magic Wallet

By Doctor What
(http://www.instructables.com/
id/Magic-Duct-Tape-Wallet/)

It's a magic wallet, made out of duct tape. The magic wallet has been done before, but I decided to make one, dirt cheap. This should last a while, and, if it gets destroyed, it only takes fifteen minutes to make another one. The story behind it: I was watching QVC, and I saw that they were selling "magic wallets" for $20 for a set of two. I thought, "Who in their right mind would pay that much for something that they can make with stuff around their house?" So, I decided to make one, on the cheap, with stuff in my bedroom. And I came up with this.

Step 1: Crap You Need

- Duct tape (for colors, go to Wal-Mart—they have every color imaginable.)

- Stiff cardboard (I used an old Converse shoebox.)
- Scissors
- Pen
- Altoid tin (trace this for wallet shape). You don't need an Altoid box specifically. You could use a playing card or anything wallet-shaped that will fit cards.

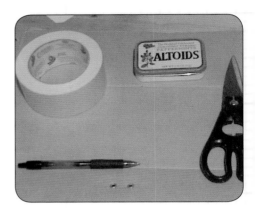

Step 2: Cut Your Cardboard

You need to trace the Altoid tin (the top, it's bigger) onto cardboard twice, then cut it out.

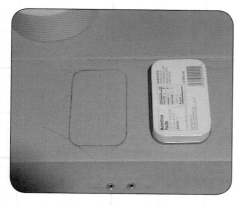

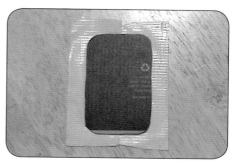

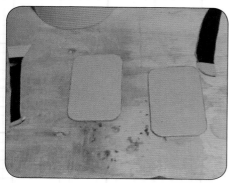

Step 4: Create Straps

Put two pieces of foot-long duct tape on top of each other to create one big strap. Then cut the big one in half, hotdog style. Then take the two strips, and cut them both hotdog-style again to get four straps.

Step 3: Cover Cardboard with Duct Tape

Cover each side of both pieces of cardboard with duct tape. Then trim the excess off of the sides. Sure, the wallet is not 100 percent duct tape; but if you don't use cardboard, it will be flimsy and won't work so well.

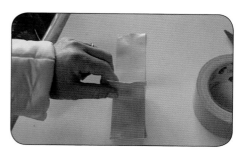

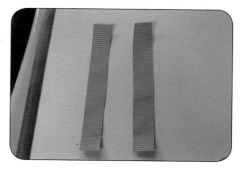

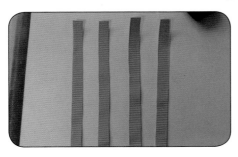

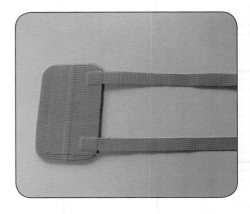

 ## Step 5: Attach Straps

You need to take two strips and attach them horizontally on one of the cards. If you are using an Altoid tin, put them between 0.5" and 0.75" from the top and bottom. Then secure them with a piece of tape. If you are not using an Altoid tin, make sure that a dollar bill's height is longer than the space in between the straps. Then, flip over the card so that the straps are on the left, under the card. Next, fold the straps over the card, so that they fit right. Place the other card on top, so that the straps are sandwiched between the two cards. Then trim the straps so that they are 0.5" to 0.75" away from the edge. Last, use a piece of tape to attach the strap ends to the back of the card on top.

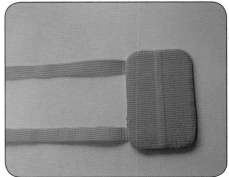

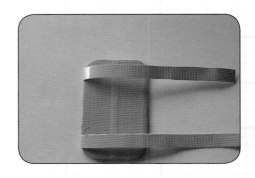

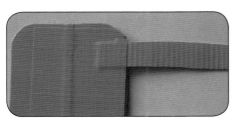

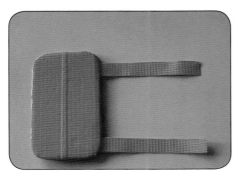

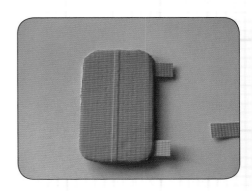

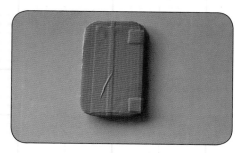

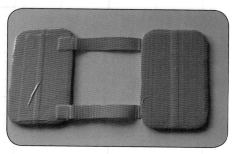

Step 6: Attach Straps
Part Deux

Now you need to attach the two other straps. Open the two cards and put the straps on the bottom card, in X formation. The two ends on the left need to go through the straps. Then place the top card on the bottom card again. Trim the ends so that the straps are, once again, 0.5" away from the edges. Make sure that the X straps do not overlap the horizontal straps, and that they are in-between the horizontal straps. Then tape the ends to the back of the cards. For the right side, tape the ends to the back card. For the left side, tape the ends to the front.

Step 7: Check Your Wallet

Get a dollar, open up your wallet, put it in, and close the wallet. Then open it from the other side. Then close it, and open it again from the side you started with.

than your card. then put some tape face down on it to cover the sticky stuff, and you have a pocket. You can make as many pockets as you want, on the front and on the back.

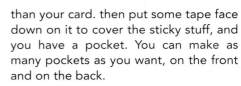

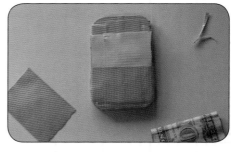

Step 8: Add Pockets

If you want pockets for your ID, credit card, etc., you need to put about 3" of tape sticky side up on your wallet. Then put another 3" strip on top of it, also sticky side up, so that you have a wide piece of tape. Make sure it is wider

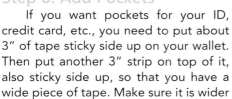

Step 9: Hooray!

You've now completed your geek wallet. Rejoice!

High-Quality Wallet

By CODO69
(http://www.instructables.com/
id/High-quality-Duct-Tape-
wallet/)

With a little time and patience, you too can make a quality duct tape wallet that's sure to impress.

Step 1: Required Materials

Roll of duct tape in your favorite color

- Quality scissors
- Ruler
- Knife or equivalent
- Packaging tape
- Paper (optional)

Step 2: Getting Started

The first step is to make the body of the wallet (the money pouch). Cut several strips of tape to the length of 10.5". The idea is to make a sheet of tape. In the first picture, it shows that two layers of tape overlap approximately halfway. Try to line up the edges as best as possible. Fold over the tape with the glue side up (picture 2). Remember these first two

steps; you'll be using them all throughout the project. Keep flipping the growing sheet over and apply strips of tape until you have a sheet that is exactly 8.5" long. Fold over the last edge like you did in step 2. Using your straight edge, score the side of the sheet (keep as close to the edge as you can). Measure the other edge and score a line that is 10 1/16" wide. Cut using your scissors.

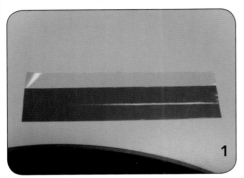

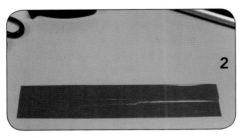

Step 3: Finishing Money Pouch

Take the finished sheet of tape and fold it in half. Using two strips of tape (4.25" long), tape the edges closed, making the pouch. When done, it should look like the picture. Set it aside (keep flat).

Step 4: Card Holders

Measure out four strips of tape measuring 3.75" long. As in the money pouch portion, line up the edges and stick the first two pieces of tape together approximately halfway. Fold over the tape that is glue side up. Using your ruler, make the length of the tape sheet exactly 2.75". Apply the fourth piece of tape and fold over the exposed edge. Repeat this step two more times. Repeat steps 1–4 once more, but instead make the length of the four tape strips 3.5". Just like with the money pouch, score the edge of the sheets to make a flush edge. Cut along the scored edges.

With your ruler, measure the three sheets of equal size to 3.375", score, and cut. Cut the one sheet that was 3.5" long to 3" even. Cut four strips of tape measuring 2.75". Place one piece over an end of each tape sheet. Cut four more pieces of tape at 2.75" long. (These next four pieces will be used to assemble the sheets together.) Lay a piece of tape across the bottom of one of the sheets (3.375") and fold the tape back so the glue side is facing up (pictures 1 and 2). I used an old credit card as a spacer so the tape folds back neatly (the yellow paper over it was to cover up any numbers on the credit cards). Stick the second sheet (3.375") on top of the first, offset by 3/8" (picture 3). Repeat the previous step with the third sheet of

3.375" and the fourth sheet measuring 3". The 3" sheet will be flush on the bottom edge of the packet (pictures 3-8). Cut a piece of tape 2.75" and place it at the bottom edge of the stack and fold it around to the back (pictures 9 and 10). If done properly, the whole thing will measure 4.25" long.

Now we have to tape the edges closed. Cut two strips of tape 4.25". I use thin strips of paper approximately 0.5" wide and 4.25" long on these two pieces of tape. They are offset approximately 0.5" from the edges. The paper is used to keep any glue from the tape from sticking to your cards. Lay the tape across the front of the packet, making sure the paper partially overlays the front side. Flip the packet over; it should look like picture 11. With your knife, make a slice at the thickest part of the packet. The slice will help keep the tape from wrinkling when you fold it over. Fold the tape over, keeping it as snug as possible (try not to wrinkle the tape). Repeat on other side with the second piece of tape. When done, your card holder should look like picture 12. Flip the packet over and cut through the tape on the front side so each individual pocket can open fully (picture 13). Repeat steps to make a second pouch. Set the two pouches aside.

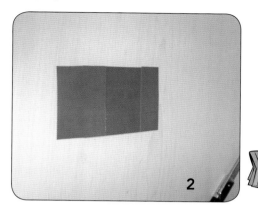

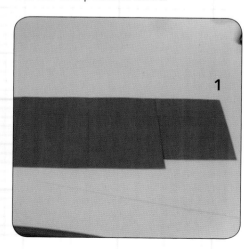

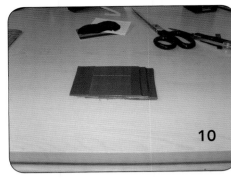

6

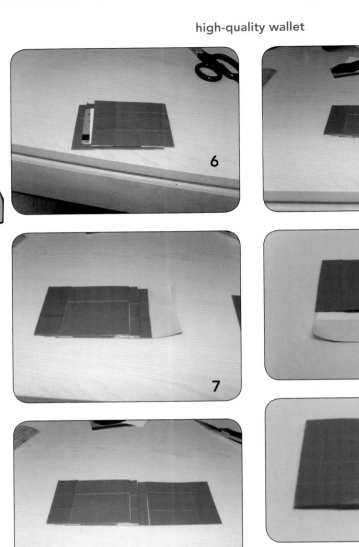

7

8

9

10

11

12

13

Step 5: Coin Pocket

Measure four strips of tape measuring 10.5" long. Like in the previous steps, overlay the tape and make a sheet that is

2.75" wide. Trim up the two outer edges, making it approximately 10" long—it doesn't need to be exact as more will be trimmed off later. Cut one piece of tape that's 2.75" long and apply it to an edge in step 4. Fold over the edge with the taped end until it's 4.125" long. With two strips of tape measuring 4.125" long, tape the pouch closed (picture 2). Set aside.

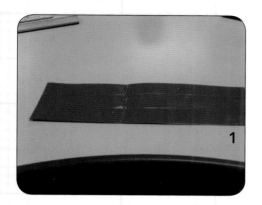

1

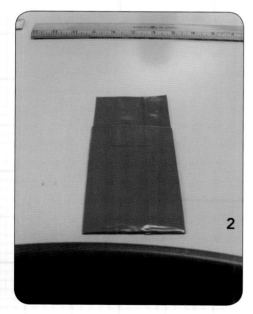

2

it so you have a straight edge. Measure the other side so the total length is 7.5" long. Cut two pieces of tape 2.75" long and apply them to the edges. Fold in half and crease the sheet. Half an inch away from all edges on one half of the sheet, make markings and cut out the square (picture 1). With your packaging tape, overlay a piece of tape on either side of the square you cut out (taping the two pieces of clear tape together). Make sure the edges of the clear tape lay on the duct tape sheet (the two outer edges will be close, but this is fine). Cut a piece of duct tape that is 3.75" long and then cut it lengthwise to a width of 1 1/16 inch. With the sheet in front of you and the section with the whole cut out on the top, apply the thin strip of tape to the right-hand side (sealing the edge and the packaging tape). Cut a piece of tape 3.75" long. With the sheet still oriented as in the previous step, flip it upside down vertically so the side with the hole is facing the bottom (flip, don't rotate). Apply the piece you just cut to the right edge (where the hole isn't; this will save you some frustration later on). Cut a piece of tape 2.75" and align it to the top edge of the whole and tape the sheet together (folded in half) (picture 2). Cut another piece of tape 3.75" long. Apply it to the left outer edge of the pouch now, sealing up the third edge to make a pouch (picture 3).

Step 6: ID Cardholder

Cut four strips of tape to 8" long. Overlay them and make the sheet 2.75" wide (like everything else . . . noticing a pattern yet?). Score one edge and cut

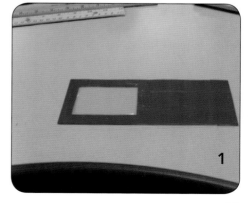

1

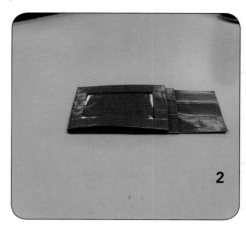

Step 7: Assembly

Take your newly made ID holder and coin pouch. Lay the ID holder on top of the coin pouch (align the bottom edges together; both pieces are 2.75" wide, so those should already be aligned), and fold the tape over that is on the ID holder. Cut a piece of tape 2.75" long and tape the bottom edges together (be sure to align the edge of the tape so it doesn't cover the ID holder window). Cut a piece of tape 3.75" long and tape the left edges together (be sure to align the edge of the tape so it doesn't cover the ID holder window). It should look like picture 2. Set aside.

Step 8: Cardholder to Money Pouch

Cut three strips of tape 2.75" long and two strips 4.25" long. Take one of the 2.75" pieces and cut it lengthwise in half. Apply one half of the 2.75" strip that you cut to the top portion of one of the cardholders. Stick the other half of the exposed tape to the inside of the money pouch (picture 2) and fold the pouch over. Take one of the other 2.75" strips of tape and tape the bottom edges of the money pouch and cardholder together. Take one of the other 4.25" strips of tape and tape the outer edges of the money pouch and cardholder together. Cut open the openings of the card slots. Repeat these steps for the second pouch on the opposite side of the wallet.

flap on the coin pouch. Fold the flap over and mark where it intersects with the ID holder. Snip the edges approximately 1/16" deep (picture 4). Take your knife or scissors and cut on an angle to your little 1/16" snips (picture 5). With your scissors, cut along the edge of where the tape ends (the piece that is attaching the flap to the money pouch). The end result should look like picture 6. Fold the flap over and tuck it behind the ID holder and . . . *you're done!*

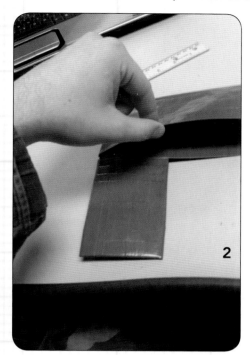

2

Step 9: ID holder/Coin Pouch to Money Holder

The final stretch! Cut a piece of tape 2.75" wide and apply it to the bottom edge of the ID/coin assembly (picture 1). Place the ID assembly in the center of the money pouch and fold over the two edges (right side then left side), and align all the edges so they are stacked evenly on top of each other (picture 2). When satisfied, fold tape over to attach the ID assembly to the rest of the wallet. Cut a piece of tape 4.25" long. Flip the ID assembly up and lay it on the table. Apply the tape to the left side of the ID (don't cover the window edge). With your knife, make a slice so the tape lays flat across the whole thing (picture 1). Press the tape to the money pouch and, if needed, tuck the extra length of tape under the left-sided cardholder (picture 1). Cut another piece of tape 2.75" (this is your last one!). Apply it approximately 0.5" down on the inside of the money pouch. Apply the rest of the tape to the

1

2

3

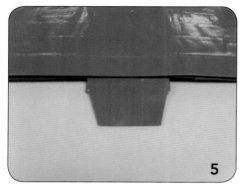

Step 10: FINISHED!

Now you've got a high-quality duct tape wallet that people will surely be envious of. This is my own design and I've sold approximately over two dozen of these wallets over the past year. I hope you enjoy it as well as everyone who has bought one from me. I've made so many that I can finish a wallet in about one and a half to two hours. If you attempt this, don't be surprised if it takes you at least twice as long (of course it was a learning process for me at first).

Stylish Wallet/ Clutch

By jerseygirl77
(http://www.instructables.com/
id/Girly-duct-tape-walletclutch/)

All of the duct tape wallets I've seen so far look like they belong in the pockets of overalls or inside a tool box. This one is a lot more feminine. It won't really fit in a pants pocket but it is a great, sturdy, everyday wallet with room for eight cards, and it is big enough that you could carry it separately as a clutch.

Materials needed

- Lots of duct tape
- Scissors
- Nail polish remover and toilet paper to clean the gunk off the scissors
- A pen/marker
- A straight edge

Step 1: Make the Base

At the base of this wallet are two sheets of duct tape. I've found that the easiest way to make one of these sheets is to start with a piece of loose leaf and cover both sides of that in duct tape. That way you can get nice straight lines. It also adds a bit more stability.

10" × 9.5"

This one needs to be folded into three sections. The first is the pocket for the cards, the second is the pocket for the money, and the third is the flap for the

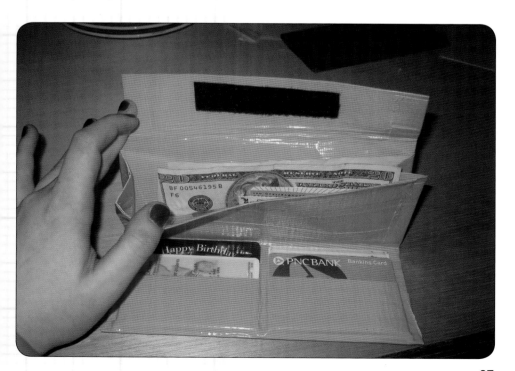

Velcro. You can see these on the finished wallet. Once you make it, fold it to the appropriate proportions. The two larger sections should be about 4" long.

4" × 9.5"

This one is taped in the middle and is part of the pocket for the money.

Step 2: Tape the Base Together

Make one strip of duct tape either by using the loose leaf or just by lining up two strips together.

Cut two lengths about 3" to 3.5" long. Fold them in half the long way and then cut them into triangles. (See the picture.) Then tape these to the short sides of the smaller sheet. Then tape the long side of the small sheet with the smaller sides of the triangles to the large sheet at the fold between the two larger sections.

Then finally tape the free sides of the triangles (in orange) to the middle section of the big sheet so that you get a pocket big enough for money.

This sounds confusing but I think the pictures make it relatively clear.

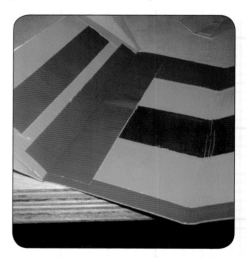

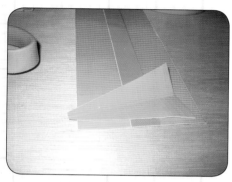

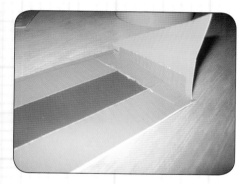

4. Slide the sleeve down again so that the folds are at the top of what will be the card pocket.
5. Take another piece of duct tape and put it over the bottom of the card pocket (sticky part out).
6. Then put that on one side of the bottom section of the big sheet, towards the top (see picture).
7. Repeat steps 1-6, except put it on the other side.
8. Then lay a piece of tape over those two pockets so that the sticky part is covered.
9. Repeat the whole thing to make another row of pockets on the bottom.

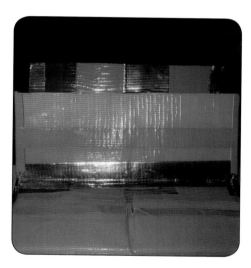

Step 3: The Card Slots

The wallet holds eight cards, but I put two in each slot so there are actually only four slots.

1. Take two cards and wrap them length wise with duct tape, sticky side out.
2. Slide the little sleeve you made down so that a reasonable amount of the card is showing (so that you would be able to grab card).
3. Make cuts on each end of the duct tape that is now sticking out over the sides. Then fold those down.

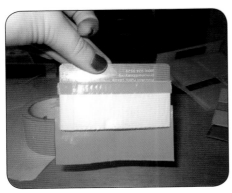

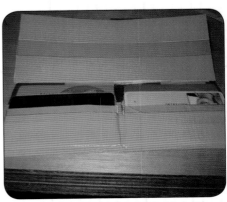

Step 4: The Finishing Touches

Add some strips or half strips to all of the exposed sides and joints just to make it sturdy and a bit prettier.

Then fold it all up and add some Velcro to the top, smallest section and to the front flap. I didn't have any Velcro on hand for this wallet but I included a picture of an old one to show the placement.

Now you've got a nice big wallet with room for plenty of cash and eight cards. This one turned out a little sloppy and the colors are a bit much, but it's for an eight-year-old so it should do.

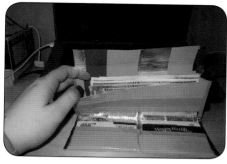

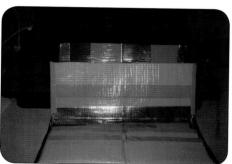

Section 3
Clothing

I was inspired to make a duct tape jacket of some kind because of hat day at my school. Why hat day, you ask? Well . . . I didn't have any awesome hats, so I made a hex hat from duct tape. It was a hit with my friends, and a lot of people gave good feedback. I was excited to do something bigger. Something with some more "wow" factor. When first worn, this jacket is kind of stiff and pretty much a plastic tube. It keeps in a *lot* of heat, and is great for wearing in the cold outside! It is also 100% waterproof, and can be used as a rain jacket. The more you wear it, the more comfortable it gets. Unlucky for me, it is still hot here in the south, even at 5:00AM when I have to go catch the bus for school.

Step 1: Materials

First, you need the right tools

- Scissors
- Razor
- Sharpie
- Yard/meter Stick

Now, gather your materials

- Duct tape. I used two 55-yard rolls, part of a 40-yard roll, and a fluorescent green tape for decorating. I probably spent around $15 for the duct tape. I didn't use professional tape—just the cheapest I could find.
- Masking tape
- A large flat surface that you can cut on. I have concrete floors, so it's no big deal. You may wish to use a large cutting board on a table if you need to (or improvise!).

Step 2: Getting Started— Duct Tape Cloth

First, we must learn how to make duct tape cloth! Making the tape can be kind of trick, but mostly just when you are covering the first layer. If two sticky parts touch in the wrong place, problems can occur. Be careful when laying down the strips! There are variations on how to make duct tape cloth, but this method works well for me and lets me get the correct size duct tape sheets I need.

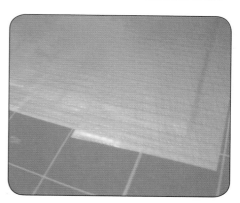

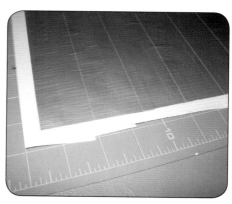

Step 3: Wait—How Big Should It Be?

See measurement chart on page 110. Now, be careful! I used the medium measurements for the body, which is 26.75" × 24". It turns out that it is *way* too wide and the jacket will be more like a tube. It is best to make the size measurement that is closest to your size, then tailor the jacket after you finish.

Step 4: Sleeves

We need to make the sleeves. I started with the sleeves because they are the easiest. Make sure you make a plain rectangle the correct width. (Mine was 9.5"−15.35" × 21.65". 21.65" was a tad short for me. Adjust to your size.)

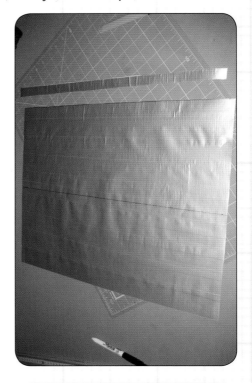

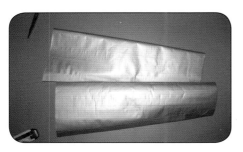

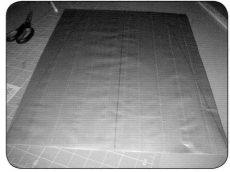

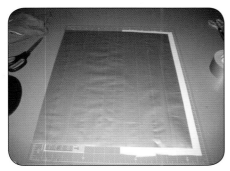

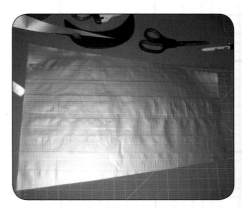

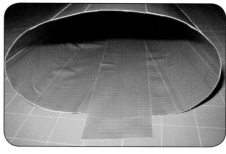

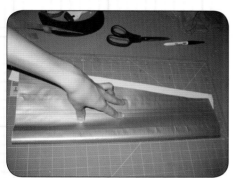

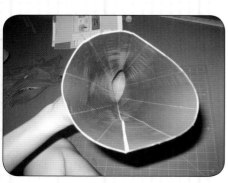

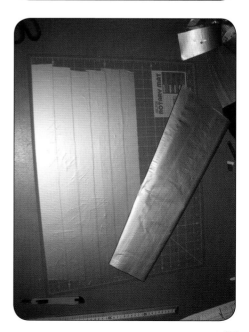

100% authentic hoodie (110+ yd of duct tape)

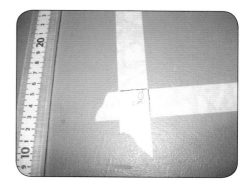

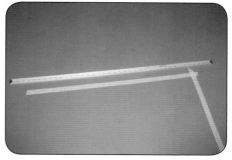

Step 5: Starting the Body

The main body is large—it did not fit on my cutting board. I used my floor to make the body, and (using masking tape, a yard stick, and a sharpie) made a large measuring angle to get the right sized duct tape cloth. If you want a zipper or a cut down the middle, make sure to measure and mark off the middle of one of the duct tape sheets.

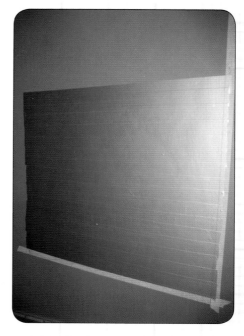

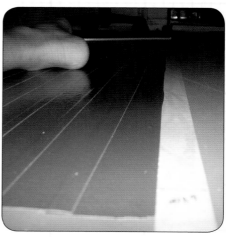

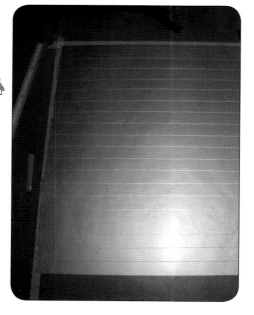

Step 6: Attaching Things

Here, we begin the end of the hoodie. The easiest way to go about attaching things is to first attach the two halves, then the sleeves, then the sides of the body. There could be another way, but I couldn't see how I was going to get duct tape strips into the enclosed area of the hoodie. The hardest part of this step is adding duct tape to the inside seem of the sleeves. It is dark inside a plastic tunnel. . . .

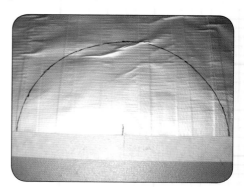

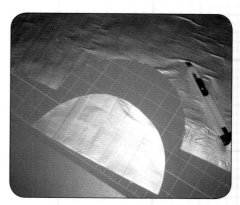

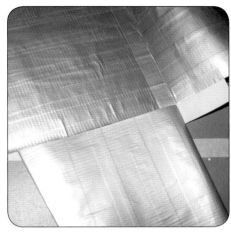

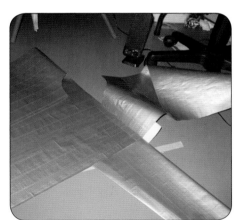

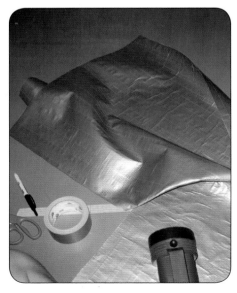

Step 7: Tailoring and Pockets!

Morning. I wake up at 5:00AM to get ready for school. I decided that since I was ready early, I would tailor the jacket and make it fit better. Afternoon. Home from school, time to work on some pockets! Because they are easy! Listen to remixes of the Tetris theme.

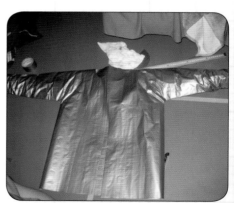

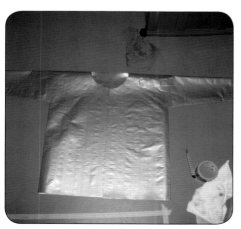

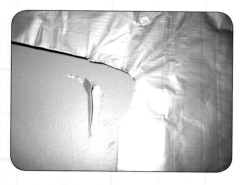

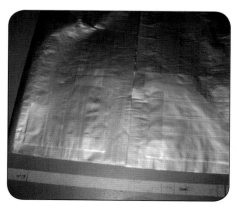

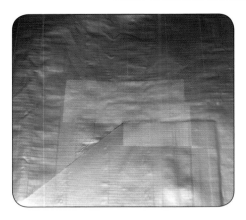

Step 8: The Long-Awaited Hood

Making the hood is pretty straightforward. All you need to do is conjoin the two rectangles and attach them to the collar of the hoodie. Trim off the top corner of the hood and round it to make it look nicer.

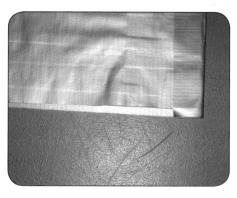

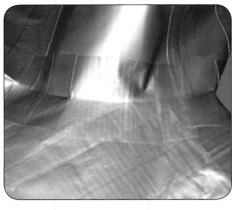

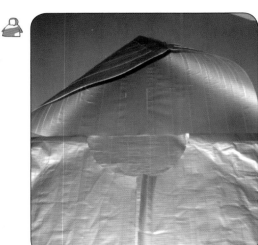

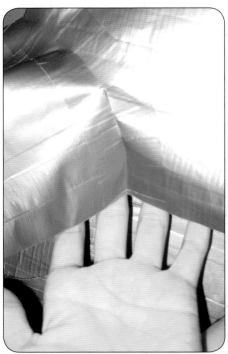

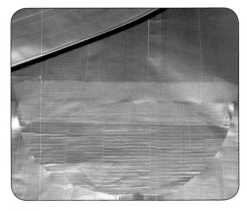

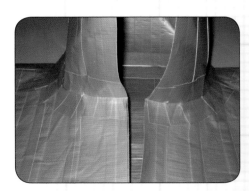

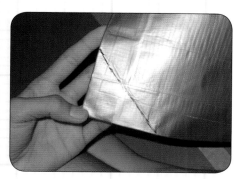

Step 9: Finishing Up!

The hoodie is technically done. But there is nothing like some colorful duct tape to make it look snazzy. You can put a bunch of stripes, checkered squares, or pictures and words with colored duct tape. I just did an easy choice and put one color of duct tape on what I consider to be borders of the jacket. After five days of work, I finished! Don't be fooled—it takes a while bit it really isn't hard. This jacket holds in a lot of heat. I mean, while taking the pictures for this in my air-conditioned room, I started sweating. It is pretty comfortable if it is cool outside with less sun. This jacket is 100% water proof also! So, if it rains while you are outside in the cold, you won't get wet! I tested this with a garden hose, and it repels very efficiently. The biggest issue is that the water drips directly onto your pants. Maybe future developments will fix this.

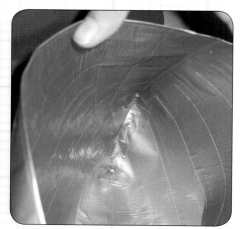

100% authentic hoodie (110+ yd of duct tape)

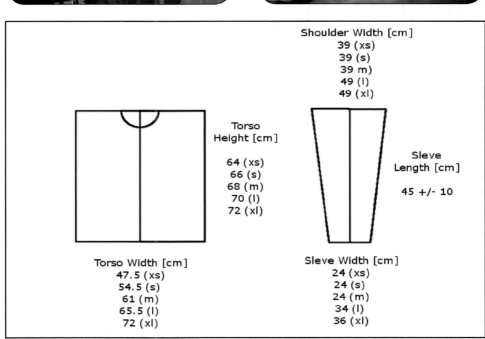

Shoulder Width [cm]
39 (xs)
39 (s)
39 m)
49 (l)
49 (xl)

Torso
Height [cm]

64 (xs)
66 (s)
68 (m)
70 (l)
72 (xl)

Sleve
Length [cm]

45 +/- 10

Torso Width [cm]
47.5 (xs)
54.5 (s)
61 (m)
65.5 (l)
72 (xl)

Sleve Width [cm]
24 (xs)
24 (s)
24 (m)
34 (l)
36 (xl)

Hiking Gaiters

By squeakykeek
(http://www.instructables.com/
id/Duct-Tape-Hiking-Gaiters/)

These hiking gaiters are easy to make and are perfect for hiking in snowy, wet, or grassy conditions.

Step 1: Supplies

- Old t-shirt
- Duct tape (2 rolls)
- Two 18" separating zippers (heavyweight)
- Thread
- Ruler
- Marker
- Sewing machine
- Sewing machine oil
- Q-tips
- Straight pins

Step 2: Forming the Gaiters

Cut the T-shirt down the middle and also through the top part of the sleeves. Wrap the T-shirt around the calf and over the top of the shoe. Tape enough to hold it in place.

Start adding strips of duct tape to leg—6" to 8" strips work best. Smooth onto the leg, the duct tape overlapping itself, and work up the entire leg. Make sure to cover shoe tops. You can cut away excess later.

111

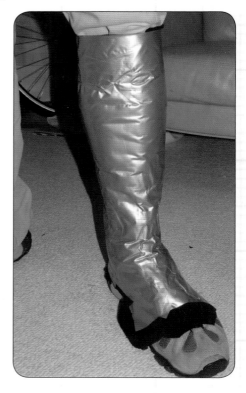

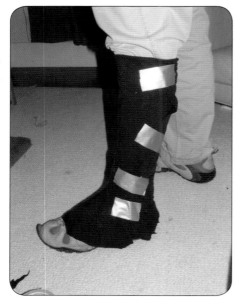

Step 3: Cutting and Edging the Gaiters

Trim the bottom to shape over the shoe. Use the ruler to draw a line down the side seam. Carefully cut through the T-shirt/tape on the line; this will be where the zipper is placed. Once off the leg, trim top and bottom to neaten and wrap all edges with duct tape. Trim away any excess T-shirt from the inside that will be flopping around.

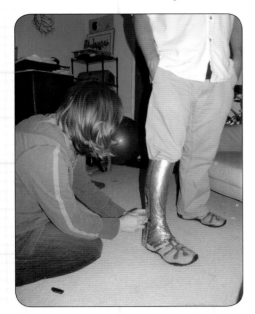

Step 4: Attaching the Zipper

Pin the zippers in place. In order to straight pin the zipper onto the gaiter, soak a Q-tip in sewing machine oil and rub the pins. This will allow the pins to easily slide through the glue on the tape. You will also need to rub the oil from the Q-tip on the sewing machine needle repeatedly to be able to sew through the duct tape without gumming up the needle. Now, sew the zippers to the gaiters.

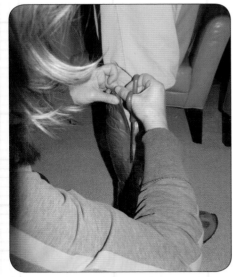

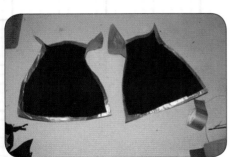

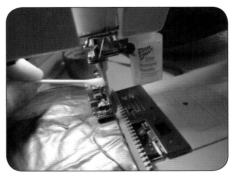

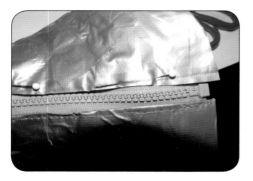

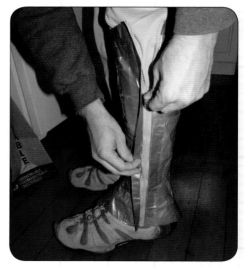

Step 5: Adding the Zipper Flap

The last step is to create an overlap with tape to cover the zipper. This will help keep moisture out. Cut a strip of tape the length of the zipper. Fold onto itself so there is only 0.5" of glue edge showing. Place the strip to the front edge of the zipper opening and reinforce the flap with another length of tape. You now have a pair of windproof, waterproof, and foxtail resistant gaiters! It also helps protect pants from Poison Oak on hikes!

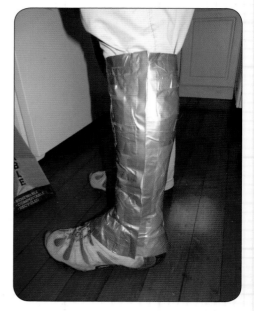

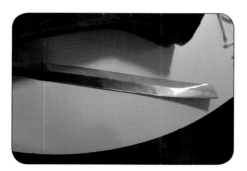

Super Fancy Waterproof/ Windproof Bike Shoe Covers

By csymmank
(http://www.instructables.com/
id/Super-fancy-waterwindproof-
bike-shoe-duct-
tape-co/)

After not seeing any good water/ windproof shoes made of duct tape in my local bike shops or online, I decided to make my own. Here is a brief write up on what I have done. This may seem to be a complicated way to make duct taped shoe covers, but it works rather nicely for me.

You will need at least one 60-yard, standard-width roll of duct tape, some scissors, a knife, and some socks. Optional is some 3M reflective tape and maybe some fastener device for the back part of the shoe. Be aware that some of the designer tapes such as zebra stripes and tie-dye come in shorter lengths, so you may want to buy two rolls. I used every last inch of my roll to make these ankle high covers.

Step 1:

Start by pulling a sock over one of the shoes and getting it tight. Be sure all the straps and such are tight enough not to interfere. The sock you use will become part of the cover, so make sure it is one you won't miss but is still in pretty good shape.

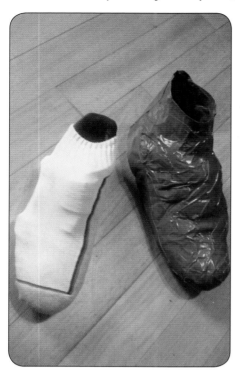

Step 3:

Here is what the back will look like after cutting the back of the sock. (I'm getting ahead but showing you a goal.)

Step 2:

Start by wrapping the toe area. Lay some short lengths over the front of the shoe. Tape may not full bond with the sock, but it should make a tight bond with other parts of tape. Try and make it smooth. Once you get a few of these done, start doing a few wraps from top to bottom and back over (if you are looking at the shoe from this perspective). Stop when you get to the cleat part of the shoe and try and leave some tread visible if you want to be able to walk on slippery surfaces.

Now, start running some strips all the way to the back. I stop at the back because I want to be able to take off my covers when I don't need to wear them. You can stop at the tongue like I did in this picture, as I cut the sock off around the hole in the shoe where your foot goes in.

Step 4:

Here is how I made the back part of the cover. I put some vertical strips here and then fold them back so they don't stick to the sock or shoe. I call this tabbing; in stagehand world, we call this a courtesy tab, i.e., "Put a courtesy tab on there so the next person can get that tape off without needing a knife to do so."

Step 5:

Here is how I started to make the ankle part of the shoe; notice it is tabbed.

Step 6:

Here is the view from the other side where I have started to make the cuff. If there is no sock on the inner part because you used low top socks like I did, then you should put tape on the inside of this piece, too.

Step 7:

Once you have the shape of the shell done, you can start carefully cutting away parts of the sock. Notice that I have folded over the tape in the left part of picture. This cut goes all the way up to just the other side of the cleat. If you are doing this part, you should also be removing the heal part of the sock and any other parts of the sock that are in the way.

Step 8:

Next, I made the bridge that keeps the cover held tight to the shoe. I put one side of tape facing out from the shoe and attached it to both insides of the shell. It should be tight enough to keep the shell close to the shop but loose enough to pull the cover off when you don't need to wear the cover.

Next I took a half-wide strip and attached it to the outside of the shell on one side. Go right down the middle of the strip and attach to the other side of the shell. Now get a knife or scissors and cut the wide strip at the edges of the shell so it can fold over the narrow strip. See the next picture for more details.

Step 9:

See! That's how the bottom of the shell will look. Now you can do the back.

Step 10:

Step 11:

This is what the back flap will look like. There is bare tape to stick to the other side of shoe. You could fancy this up with Velcro, snaps, or even a zipper, but this is my low effort way of making this work.

Step 12:

Last thing to do is to style your covers out. I used 3M reflective tape and a sharpie to make these sweet graphics. Have fun with this and maybe try and imitate the style of some popular $300 bike shoes. You could have some high end gear heads geeking out on your high end shoes and maybe even get invited to some serious rides regardless of your bike or how sweet your jersey is.

Other things you might do is put a neoprene collar at the top to prevent water from dripping down into shoes or maybe some cool fur liners.

Typhoon Pants

By Stuart Sweeney Smith
(ATTILAtheHUNgry)
(http://www.instructables.com/
id/Duct-tape-Typhoon-
Pants/)

The rainy season has come early this year in Japan, and with it—typhoons. As a person who relies on my bike as my sole means of transportation, having a good set of rain gear is crucial to arriving anywhere dry. Unfortunately, my cheap $1 rain pants ripped open on my first ride out. Clearly it was time for me to step up my game.

And what better way to stay dry than with a pair of duct tape pants? And not just your everyday rain-pants; these puppies are full-on *typhoon*-pants, with a cinched waist, cinched legs, and a front pocket, all 100% duct tape.

Making these pants was a bit of a learning process (my largest duct tape project prior to this was my wallet), and my photos don't do a good job of showing the trial-and-error sequence of events. Anyone trying to make a pair of these will probably hit similar problems and find their own solutions, so this Instructable will just give the basics, and I'll leave the particulars to you guys.

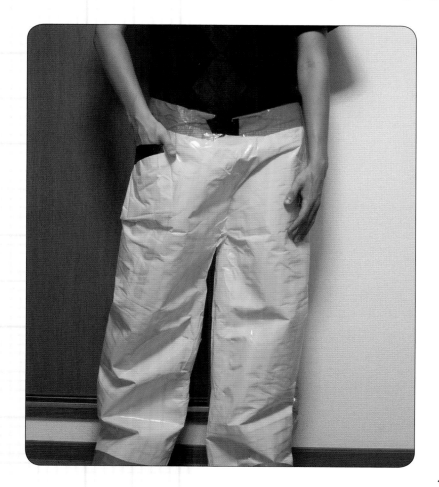

Step 1: Gather Your Duct Tape

To make these pants, I used five complete 50-foot rolls of duct tape, half of three more rolls, and a bit of a fourth, for a grand total of about 330 ft of tape—or a little over a football field. I used four colors:

- Red – interior lining
- Yellow – exterior surface
- Silver – structural elements
- Black – trim

I also used scissors for clean cuts.

Step 2: Ruin a Terrible Pair of Pants

This Instructable was inspired by the catastrophic failure of my original dollar-store rain pants a few weeks ago. But rather than throw them away, I decided to cut them open and use them as a template for my duct tape design. I drew a chalk outline (actually a duct tape outline) around the pants and created a design template on the floor of my apartment.

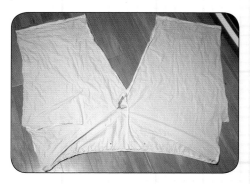

Step 3: I Make My Pants One Leg at a Time, Just Like Everybody Else

The next step is to begin putting your tape down over your template. I did this starting with the interior layer. I began laying horizontal strips of the red duct tape from the waist down, proceeding until I reached the end of the first leg. (Obviously this is done with the sticky side up.) I only did one leg at a time, partly because I wanted to practice my technique before starting the second leg, and partly because it was easier to reach parts of the pants with only one leg getting in my way. I added a few vertical strips in the seat of the pants, which is where I figured the most wear and stress would occur while biking.

The next step is to add your pockets. I had originally planned on having two, or even four pockets, but they were so time consuming that I ended up leaving off at just one. I don't have many pictures

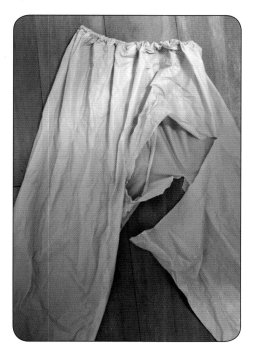

of this process, but in essence a pocket is just a square of duct tape, sealed on three sides, with the smooth side in and the sticky side out. Then you stick it to the rest of the pants.

This is also the step where you can begin planning where your cinch cord loops will be going.

Step 4: Weatherproofing (Plus the Second Leg)

Next I added the exterior layer, which will shield me from the elements. This layer doesn't have to be canary yellow, but honestly, why wouldn't it be?

I began layering strips of yellow tape vertically to add structural support to the horizontal strips in the interior. This is also the step where I finished the cinch loop on the leg and almost finished the loop at the waist. Then I repeated the previous steps in making the second leg. Since the legs have a bit of overlap, I curled the edge of the first leg and stuck it temporarily to itself, to keep the legs from getting tangled.

Step 5: Roll It on Up

The final step is to roll your pant legs closed, followed by the waist, and seal them up. For this, flip the pants over so the exterior (yellow) side is facing down, and begin by rolling just one leg closed. Use the excess tape at the edges to stick them together. Repeat this process with the second leg, again sticking everything together (roughly at first) with the excess tape along the edges. It will still look rough.

Lastly, finish the pants by covering any excess stickiness and filling any gaps with nice yellow finishing tape. Cover the rim of the pocket, and the holes of your cinch bands with some black trim tape. Now you've got a sweet pair of Typhoon pants, ready to take you through the storm as dry as can be.

typhoon pants

Hat

By Glenn Bukowski (oldsod)
(http://www.instructables.com/
id/Duct-Tape-Hat-3/)

Tools
- Scissors
- Stapler
- Marking pen

Supplies
- Newspaper
- Corrugated cardboard
- Two-liter soda bottle
- Rolls of duct tape (one each of silver, red, white, and blue)
- A hat to copy (I worked with a military-style cap)

The first part of the project is to develop patterns from the hat. The military-style cap I chose is simple—basically a low cylinder made from a strip of material, an oval top, and a short bill.

Start by tracing the brim onto the cardboard. If you don't have your own hat to copy, print out the pictures that I posted in this Instructable to make your own pattern (that's why I labeled them with their dimensions and photographed everything on a 1" × 1" grid).

The dimensions I used for the oval top of the hat and the two side pieces are labeled in the third picture on this page.

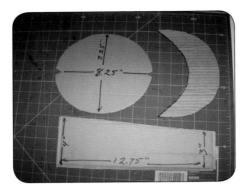

Step 1: Sheets of Silver Duct Tape

Lay strips of duct tape on the newspaper, overlapping the strips by about 0.25" to make sheets of material. One sheet will be about 9" × 10" (the top) and the other will be about 9" × 13" (the two-sided pieces). The silver duct tape will be the inside lining of your hat.

Trace the top of the hat onto the smaller piece of sheet. Notice the notches. They are there to identify the longest dimension of the oval and help you orient it when you attach it to the side of the hat. When you lay out the two side pieces, make sure that they are mirror images of each other.

Trace the bill pattern onto the side of a two-liter soda bottle with your marker and cut it out.

You'll cover the top of the plastic bill (convex side) with blue duct tape. Neatness counts!

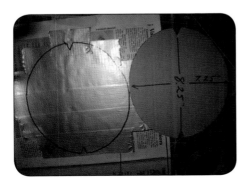

Step 2: Assemble the Sides

Now you have all the basic pieces of the hat with duct tape on one side. We'll start assembly by attaching the two side pieces together at their narrow ends. Put them together paper side (outside) to paper side then "sew" them together with a stapler.

Open them out—paper side down—and flatten the seam. Cover the stapled seam with a piece of duct tape to cover any sharp edges.

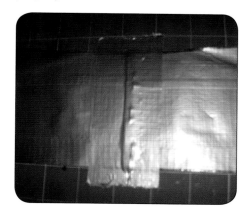

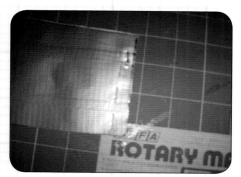

Step 3: Red, White, Blue outside

Now, the stuff that will show:

On the newspaper side of the hat, place white and red stripes of duct tape. After you've trimmed back the raw edges of the tape, place a blue strip of tape (outside hat band) at the bottom of the piece. It should overhang the sides by a little less than half its width so you can fold it over to the inside.

Next the top. (I covered the outside of the oval top with white tape.) Line up the notch marks of the oval with the front and back seams of the hat side and staple them in place. Then continue around the sides. (Tip: I staple halfway between the front and back staples, then halfway between the middle and the front, then halfway between that and the next, etc. Makes for neater work than trying to staple in sequence all around.)

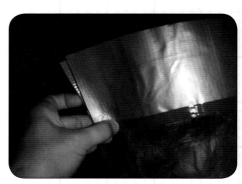

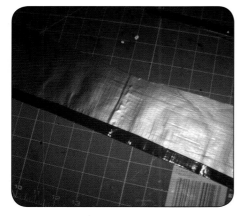

Step 4: Sizing and Assembly

Now, to the final steps:

With the side inside out, place the hat on your head and pinch the ends together to mark the seam location with your thumbnail. Staple the sides together on that pinch line. Flatten the seam out and cover it with a piece of tape.

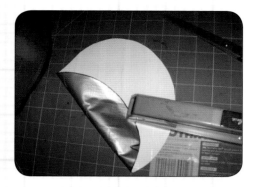

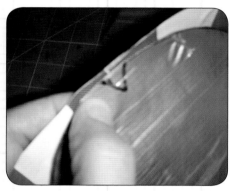

Step 6: Attach the Bill

Cover the inside of the bill (concave side) with tape. Trim the tape in front, even with the plastic form, but leave the back overhang by an inch or so. Make slits in the overhanging tape in back so it can bend up without too many wrinkles. Attach the bill to the crown of the hat, making sure the center of the bill is aligned with the front seam.

(We're almost done.)

Step 5: Right-Side Out (Finally)

Now flip the hat right-side out. (So easy to say—take your time, here. This step will tell you if you have any weak points in your construction.) You start with the silver side out, end up with the red, white, and blue side out.

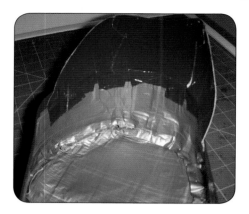

Step 7: Final Assembly

Cut a 24" strip of tape and fold it a half-inch or so over, this will be the inner hat band. Middle the tape and start attaching it to the hat from the center front to the back on one side, then the other. You should have some overlap at the back of the hat.

Try it on. If your hat feels too loose, you can add another layer of tape to the inside hat band.

OPTIONAL STEPS

You can put a decoration on the top. (I made a star from blue tape—too much white showing otherwise.)

You might want to take a leather punch and cut some vent holes around the side. Remember that duct tape is waterproof and a little air-flow is a good thing.

Step 8: FINISHED!

The tie-dye hat is the one I made for my wife. Try one and use your imagination for color combos!

Section 4

Tech

The Best Universal, Portable Videogame Holster Ever

By mason0190
(http://www.instructables.com/
id/The-Best-Universal-
Duct-Tape-Portable-
Videogame-Ho/)

I just bought four rolls of duct tape, and needed something to do with it. My little brother was bugging my dad for a new 3DS case, so a little light bulb went off in my head, and I got right to work! Average time: 45 min–1 hr.

Step 1: Materials
You will need
- A primary duct tape color (referred to here on in as Tape A)
- A secondary duct tape color (referred to here on in as Tape B)
- Console, games, and, in this case, a stylus
- Pen and paper
- Velcro dots (two is enough)
- OPTIONAL: something to cut the tape with. I used my hands and found it to be easier.

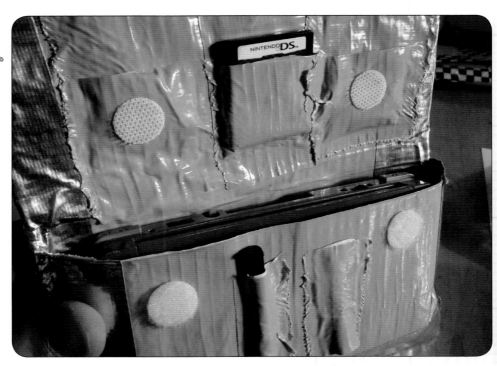

Step 2: Take Some Measurements

Make some measurements of whatever you need to hold. Try to keep it wider rather than thinner, so there's a little wiggle room. The stylus is not as important, as we will only make a small holster/slot for it.

Step 3:

Use enough of Tape A to cover about 2.5 times the length (top to bottom) of the console, and make a sort of "cloth." Five pieces were enough for me. Don't worry about the ends not being perfect, we'll cover those up later. Place more tape on the cloth, sticky side to sticky side, to make a duct tape cloth, so to speak. Then, fold lengths of Tape B over the sides to A) cover up the ragged edges and B) make it look cool. It should loosely hold the console folded over, with plenty of overhang.

Step 4: Make Game Slots

Make a small piece of duct tape loosely the dimensions of the game, with about the width of two pennies on any side. Then, use a larger piece to cover it. There should be a U-shape of stickiness around a cloth portion. Stick that on the case, with the open end at the top. Continue until you reach the desired number of slots. My brother wanted six, so I made six slots in a 3" × 2" rectangle.

131

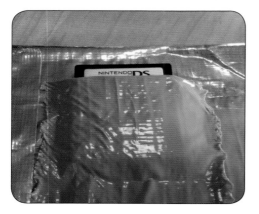

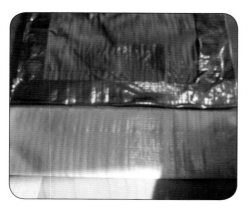

Step 6: Add Tape and Attach

Put some of Tape B on all but one long side of the newly made cloth, as depicted. Fold the tape over on the body to attach the pocket to the body. This is where the console goes.

 ## Step 5: Make Another Cloth Section

This one took me about two pieces lengthwise. Make it about 0.5" longer than the body on each side.

Step 7: OPTIONAL: Stylus Holder

Make a thin strip of tape (use the width of the roll as a length guide. 0.5" should be enough. Then, make another about 0.75" in length. Stick the small one sticky side to sticky side on the other. Stick it to the main pocket. I made two.

Step 8: Add a Little Flair

Down the middle, over Tape A, put a length of Tape B. Don't cover the edges (already covered with Tape B). Over those edges, cover with Tape A. Use the picture as a guide.

Step 9: Add Velcro Dots/ Strips

This is to ensure that nothing falls out. Note: Put the first dot on the top so you don't accidentally cover up the game pocket like I did.

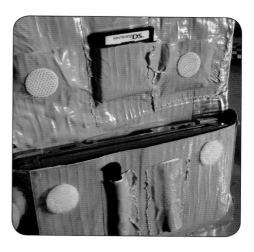

Step 10: Final Product!

Fill the case with your swag and it's done! Also available in PSP flavor.

Laptop Skin

By hummer_head
(http://www.instructables.com/
id/Duct-tape-laptop-skin/)

When you have a laptop, the concept of portability means scratches and bruises. When they become more obvious than the laptop's logo, it's getting a little bit ugly. When this happens, it's probably time to get a skin—or why not make a skin? I already had a skin on my laptop, but it was a year old—I needed a change. So this is what I came up with.

Step 1: Materials

This project is very cheap and easy. All you need is one black and one white roll of duct tape (or any other colors of your choice).

Step 2: The Background

Before I could start, I had to answer one of the biggest questions known to mankind: Is the zebra white with black stripes or black with white stripes?

Step 3: Zebra Stripes

Just sticking the white tape on the background wasn't good enough. I had to shape the pieces in unequal white stripes.

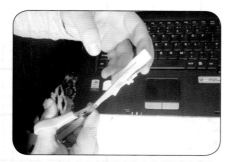

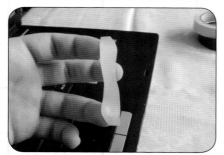

Step 4: And so on

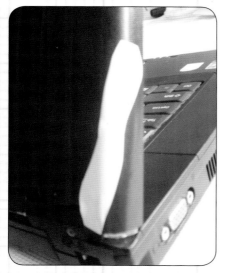

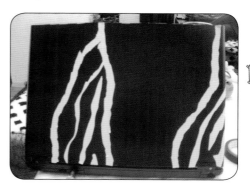

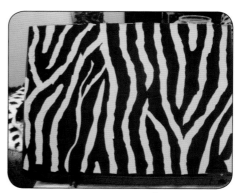

I have seen a few duct tape laptop case Instructables, but they either involved modifying a jiffy bag (which is a good idea but just didn't look pretty or neat enough for me personally) or included cardboard for the main padding and protection for the laptop (which doesn't look like it would protect it enough for me. I would always be paranoid it would break in my bag). So I have to admit, I stole my ex-boyfriend's idea of using bubble wrap for the padding.

Step 1: Materials

You will need

- The laptop you want to make the case for
- One roll of duct tape in the color you want (I used black to match the laptop)
- Scotch-tape
- Bubble wrap
- Sharp scissors
- Paper

Note: The duct tape tends to gum up the scissors, so wipe them between cutting each piece to keep the edges clean, or the duct tape tends to fray and stay sticky or come unglued.

The total cost for everything I needed was 6.

Step 2: Making the Padded Wallet for the Case

Measure out your bubble wrap. It needs to be long enough to double up, so you get a double layer of padding, and then long enough to wrap around the laptop.

I taped the join in the middle so that it wouldn't make the edges of the case rough.

Place the laptop at one end and use it to tape the edges down; you are effectively making an envelope for the laptop. Note: Be careful at this point to not tape it too tight or you won't be able to get the laptop back out, let alone when it gets tighter when the duct tape is added.

Check that you can remove the laptop. It's now ready for the next stage.

Step 3: Duct Tape!

Take your paper and fold it up to make something to add to either side of the laptop. This will ensure that you can pull the duct tape tight when wrapping but not too tight that the laptop won't come back out again.

Start at the bottom by covering the underside in one strip and folding the excess up to form neat edges.

Then start wrapping duct tape around one "line" at a time.

Continue until you reach the line before the lip of the case. Now, to edge the lip nicely, take a strip and place it halfway on the inside of the case, and then wrap it around to cover it nicely. Once this bit has been done, add in the last line of tape to finish it neatly.

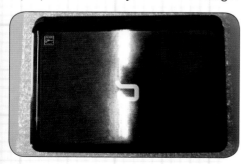

Step 4: The Finishing Touches

Now, to finish off the case, you will need a flap of some sort to cover the opening. This can be any size. You can make a short one that is held down with Velcro or a long one that wraps around. For this, I made a long one so it doesn't need anything to keep it held down. To do this it is made exactly the same as the "body" of the case. Wrap the tape around line by line until it reaches the appropriate length you require. Then, take your scissors and trim the edge so that it is straight with no loose bits.

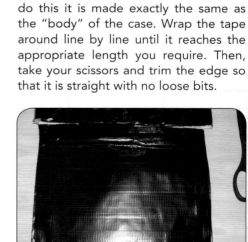

Hydraulic Robot

By Nelson_Yepez
(http://www.instructables.com/
id/Hydraulic-robot-made-of-
cardboard-and-scotch-duct-/)

I've always wanted to do this project, but, in all the guides, I always found that you need some kind of wood cutting skills and/or tools. So, I decided to make a simple hydraulic robot with cardboard, reinforced and held by duct tape that, anyone can do. Duct tape not only is strong, but also looks pretty cool; it gives the robot a cool metal like look and it holds everything together really well.

Step 1: What You are Going to Need!

For the Body of the Robot

- Cardboard box (the harder the better—I used a pizza box, but you can use any type as it will be reinforced with the duct tape.)
- Scotch duct tape (I like the silver because of the metal-like look.)
- 3 machine screws 3" in size with nuts
- 2 machine screws 1.25" in size with nuts
- A flat and square piece of wood, ideally 12" × 12", for the base to attach the robot to

For the Hydraulic System

- 8 syringes (You can get them at any pharmacy without prescription. Just say you need the type that is used

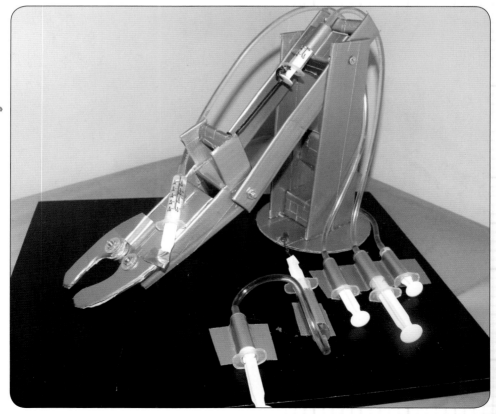

for cough medicine. I got mine at CVS and Walgreens for free.)
- 6 ft of clear tubing 0.25" × 0.17"
- Water

TOOLS
- Scissors
- Ruler
- Pen
- Drill

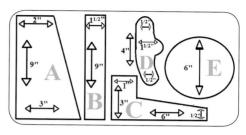

Step 2: Draw the Template

Now draw the template on the cardboard. The pictures show the measurements that I used, but you can change them to make a smaller or bigger robot. From the template cut out:
- 2 × A piece
- 2 × B piece
- 2 × C piece
- 2 × D piece
- 1 × E piece

These are the main parts of the body. The rest of the parts are going to be made as you go, because they depend on the thickness of your cardboard and how many layers of duct tape you use. Because I used a thick pizza box, I only needed one layer.

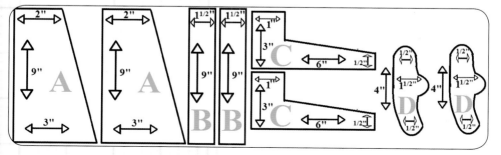

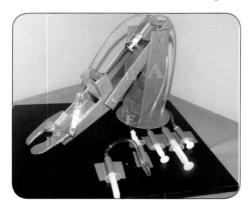

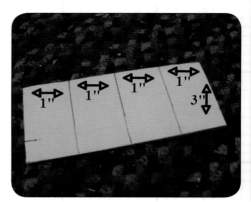

Step 3: Reinforce Your Parts

Now that you have all of your parts cut out, you have to reinforce them. First cover one side of a piece with duct tape, then cut the extra tape, cover the other side, and cut the extra tape.

Repeat this for all the parts. If your cardboard is not strong enough, repeat this step, putting on more layers of tape until you are satisfied with your result.

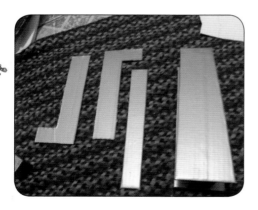

Step 4: Start Building

Now the best part—when you see your robot starting to take shape.

The next piece you have to make is a cube that is going to hold together the bottom of the two A pieces. For my robot, I used a cube that is 3" wide with 1" sides (a cube equals four sides). After you cut and fold the cube, reinforce it with tape.

Step 5: Continue Building

The reinforced cube needs to be attached to the bottom of the A piece (the bottom is the longer part).

First attach it to one piece and then the other. Put your piece on the floor to make sure the cube is level before taping. The technique I use is something I call "L taping." Look at the picture so you can understand better. Next attach the A+CUBE+A piece to the 6" circle base using L taping (use as much tape as you think is necessary to get a strong hold).

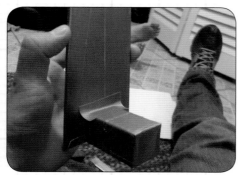

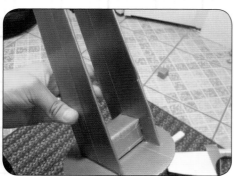

Step 6: Make Your Next Cube and Holder for the First Syringe

Hold your two B pieces on the inside of the A+CUBE+A piece and measure the space between them—that is how wide your cube needs to be. Now make your cube with your new size following step 4 (in my case, my new cube is 2.5" wide). Keep the 1" measure for the sides of the cube.

After making your cube, attach it to the B piece, leaving 1" of space from the end. Next, depending on the thickness of your cardboard, make two or more squares as wide as your first cube (in my case 3") by 1" long and tape them together. This will be taped to the middle of the A+CUBE+A piece to hold the syringe. Place the square vertical and give it just a little an angle.

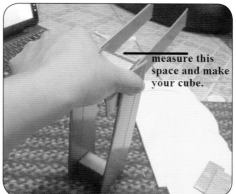

measure this space and make your cube.

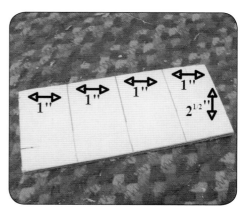

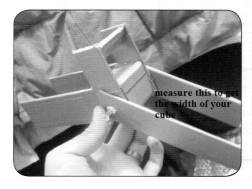

measure this to get the width of your cube

3"

1"

Step 8: Make the Holder for the Claw and the Claw

Now you have to make the holder for the claw that goes between the C+CUBE+C piece. The holder is a rectangular cube that is 4" long and the sides are 2" × 0.5". Follow the same steps in step 4, and then attach it to the front of the C+CUBE+C piece, flush with the front.

Now make the claw: the D piece. Depending on the thickness of your cardboard, you need to put enough layers of cardboard and tape to get a strong claw (in my case, two layers of cardboard and one of tape).

Make holes in both parts of the claw large enough for your 1.25" screw. Now make a hole in the front corner of the claw holder in the C+CUBE+C piece. Put your screws in and attach the claw parts. At this point, you should be halfway there. Hold the parts in their place and drill. You have to drill in the joints of the robot across the inside of the cubes, and then place your screws.

the angle is more something like this

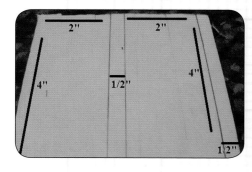

2" 2"

4" 1/2" 4"

1/2"

Step 7: Build Next Part and Next Cube

Repeat the beginning of step 6, but with the C pieces. Hold your C pieces on the inside of the B+CUBE+B piece and measure the space between them. That is how wide your cube needs to be (in my case 2" wide) by 1" long for the sides. Reinforce the cube and then attach it to the corner of the C pieces.

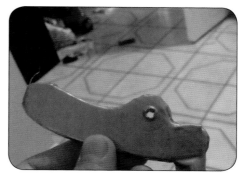

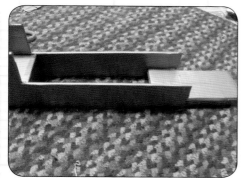

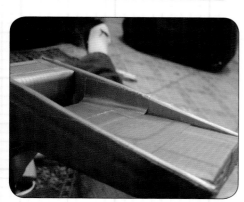

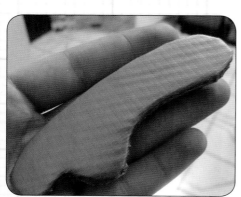

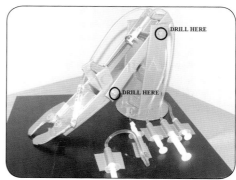

Step 9: Attach to Base and Make Hydraulic System (First Syringe)

Now, attach the robot to the base. Drill in the middle of the cube at the bottom of the A+CUBE+A piece and on the wood for the base and place your 3″ screw.

Now, begin building the hydraulic system. Attach your first syringe to your holder on the A+CUBE+A piece (just like the picture). Now, cut two pieces as wide as your second cube by 0.5″ and tape them together. Attach this to the 1″ space you left in the B+CUBE+B piece (just like the picture). Then put a pin in that new piece and tape around it. Tightly tie a piece of rope to the pin and, from there, to the syringe. Make sure the arm is down and the syringe is all the way out to get the right length of your rope (refer to picture for better understanding).

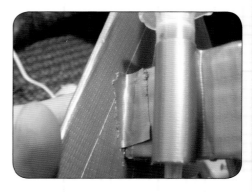

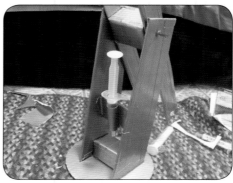

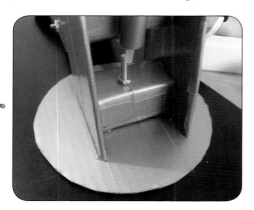

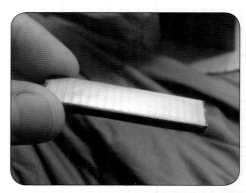

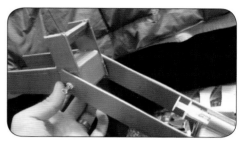

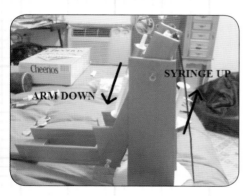

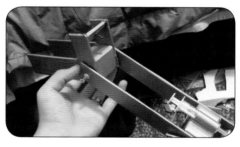

Step 11: Syringe for the Claw

The syringe for the claw is going to be directly attached to the claw with duct tape. Make sure the duct tape is not too tight so the claw can move freely.

Step 10: Second Syringe

For the second syringe, you need to make a holder in the top part of the C+CUBE+C piece. Use the same procedure as step 9. Make sure the arm is down and the syringe is out to get the right length for the rope. This is completely adjustable depending on how high or how low you want your arm to move. Play around with the length of the rope to find out what works best for your robot.

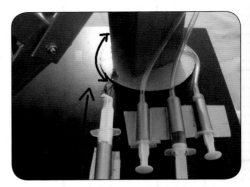

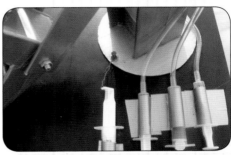

Step 13: Run the Tubing to All Syringes

Run the tubing to all the syringes, fill with water, and enjoy.

Step 12: Syringe to Turn the Arm

At the base of the robot, attach a pin and the syringe about 3" from the pin. Attach a wire from the pin to the syringe so that, when the syringe moves, it makes the arm rotate left or right. Now tape three syringes to the wood base next to each other. Each of these is to be connected to the syringes in the arm.

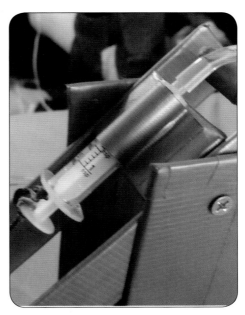
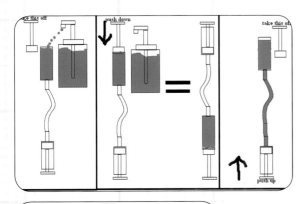
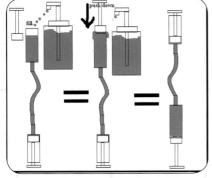

149

Section 5
Home & Furniture

Hammock

By Dadzilla
(http://www.instructables.com/
id/Duct-Tape-Hammock-1/)

This red, white, and blue hammock is the perfect place to relax on the Fourth of July!

Step 1: The Pieces

- Three rolls of Scotch duct tape
- Two wooden dowels (48" × 1" diameter)

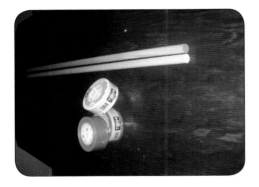

Step 2: The Setup

Since this hammock is woven, and duct tape is as sticky as, well, duct tape, a rigid set-up is necessary. I used a wooden table I had built, screwed 2" × 4" scraps (12" long) to the sides, then attached the dowel with another screw. The distance between the points of attachment of the dowel will be slightly more than your hammock width. My final width was about 34".

Step 3: Long Loops

Roll tape out sticky-side up and run it under dowels on each end.

Step 4: Folding Over

Press tape down onto itself on one side, and then roll out enough tape to complete the loop and press the loop together.

Step 5: Lots of Long Loops

Continue making loops, close but not touching, until full width is reached. Stagger the tape joints.

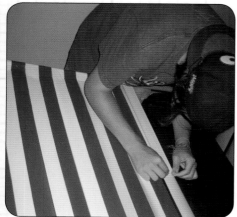

Step 6: Marking for Weaving

The important thing to remember before starting to weave is that the side facing up is the bottom. Take a ruler and mark where the tape edges go on the outer two loops of each side of the hammock. To duplicate my pattern, start on the outside with a mark about 2" from the end, then make a mark every 7.5". Move to the inside loop and make a mark 5.75" from the end, then make marks every 7.5".

Step 7: Weaving

I used a piece of 0.5" PVC (you could use a broom handle) to separate my loops, then I used the ruler as a shuttle to pass between them. Making these loops is the same as before—sticky side up, then fold over. Be careful not to pull the outside loops in when you fold over.

Step 8: Weave Setup

Be careful when weaving duct tape; it will hang up given half a chance.

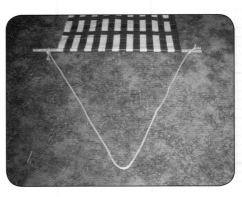

Step 9: Bottom Side of the Weave

When weaving is finished, it will look like this. Remember, at this point the bottom side is still up. Only the top side of the loop is woven. The bottom side (visible here) is stuck down all the way across. Also notice how the weaves shift up and down. This is because I have an even number of long loops. With an odd number it would shift inside and out.

Step 11: Securing the Hangers

You wouldn't want the ropes to slip, so secure them with . . . wait for it . . . duct tape! Tape over the dowel, the knot, and then the dowel on the other side of the knot.

Step 12: Enjoy!

Find some suitable trees, hang the hammock, and relax . . . or fake relaxing, like my son in the picture.

Step 10: Attach Rope

Make a triangular rope support for each end of the hammock. The length of the rope will be approximately 10 ft and tied to the hammock on either side.

Stars and Stripes Lawn Chair

By Kapaow
(http://www.instructables.com/
id/Stars-and-Stripes-Duct-Tape-
Lawn-Chair/)

We decided to fix up my grandmother's old lawn chair for the 3M Duct Tape Contest.

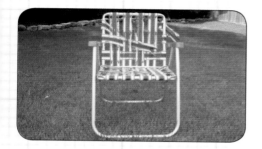

Step 1: Clean Up the Chair

Cut off all the old straps and wipe off the aluminum with a damp rag.

Step 2: Preparation

We used a rust-proof, hammered-bronze spray paint finish. We applied several thin coats, making sure it did not run.

Step 3: Making the Straps

Measure the width of the chair and add about 3", which will allow 1.5" on each side for the tape to wrap around the post. Stick it, sticky side up to two secure places (not on the chair). This step is to layer the tape to make it strong enough to sit on and to cover the sticky side. Make sure it's tight. Then place another layer of tape (sticky side to sticky side, leaving 1.5" on each end uncovered) on top of the strips. Make sure it is aligned correctly. Once centered, slowly run your finger along the tape to stick them together. Be sure to remove as many air bubbles as possible. Repeat this step on the top and bottom to attain the desired strength. (More layers equal more strength and less stretch.) We did three layers.

Step 4: Putting It Together

We did all the red, horizontal strips first, and then we wove the white and one blue strip through them. Make sure your straps are tight and evenly spaced. All vertical straps go under the metal bar in the back.

Step 5: FINISHED

We can't wait to present our grandmother with her "new" duct tape chair on the Fourth of July so she can sit and enjoy the fireworks in stars and stripes style!

Patio Pillow

By Lauren Ryder

(annahowardshaw)

(http://www.instructables.com/
id/Quilty-Duct-Tape-PatioLawn-
Pillow/)

Cozy up your patio furniture or picnic blanket with quilt-inspired, weatherproof pillows! This project is super quick, inexpensive, and provides an attractive alternative to the standard (and generally hideous) outdoor decor.

Materials and Tools

This project requires very few materials, but can be as complex as you like. All you need is:

- Duct tape—preferably a heavy/weatherproof tape, as the structural front and back pieces (which I am going to call the "base tape"), and then as many colors as you need for your pattern
- One-gallon freezer bag
- Packing peanuts
- Rotary cutter (or other cutting implement)
- Cutting mat with length indicators—this does not need to be a cutting mat. However, you do need a surface on which you can easily attach and remove duct tape. Length markers of any kind will be really helpful for lining things up.

Step 1: Tape Base

Start by making and attaching the back of the pillow to the freezer bag:

- Lay out seven slightly overlapping strips of base duct tape, about 12" long.
- Remove and flip the whole piece over.
- Place the freezer bag in the center.
- Fold the outlying tape over both sides and the bottom of the bag
- Along the top, fold the tape over on itself, not interfering with the zipper.

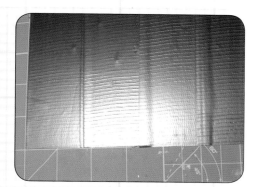

Step 2: Tape Triangles

For this particular pillow, I made 32 triangles using three different colors. Since this is a pretty straightforward pattern, I did not chart it out in any way. If you want to do something more intricate, you might to want to grab some graph paper and do a little more planning than I did.

To make triangles

- Lay out a 3" strip of colored duct tape.
- Fold it at the middle at a 90 degree angle.
- Fold over the sides.
- Fold over the remaining small triangles.

159

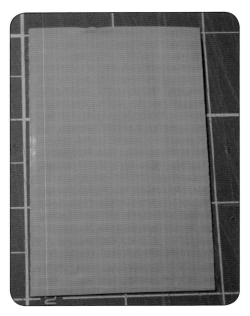

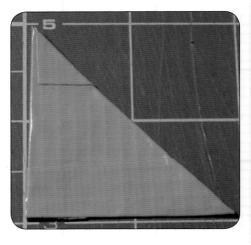

Step 3: Lay Out

Lay out all your triangles in the way that you want the final piece to look and confirm that you have all the pieces you need and that everything is going to line up. Take a moment to think about how cute this will be when completed, how much faster this is than real quilting, and if duct tape is allowed in the Amish culture.

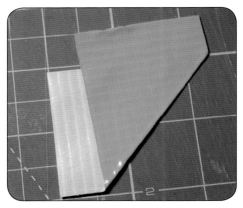

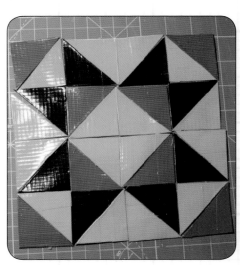

Step 4: Tape Triangles

The front panel is created by taping down one column of triangles at a time and then connecting the separate columns into the full panel. Trying to do the whole

thing at once on a single large piece would surely end in disaster.

- Unroll a 10" piece of base tape.
- Lay it on the mat sticky side up.
- Carefully set the pieces of tape in order of the pattern.
- Ever so slightly, overlay the blue tape on the pieces around it. Just a teeny, tiny bit. This will not only make it look a little more like a quilt, but it will prevent any sticky part of the tape from peeking through on the final product.
- Line up the columns.
- Flip and tape everything together.

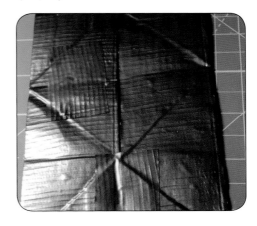

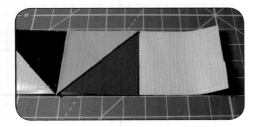

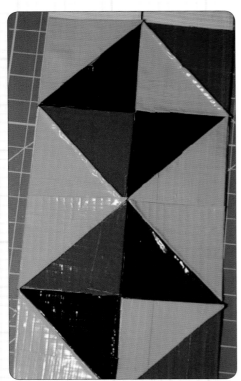

Step 5: Edging

Time to add edging!

- Unroll four 10" pieces of base tape.
- Fold them in half, width-wise.
- Unroll four more 10" pieces of base tape.
- Place a piece of tape (from second set) under the bottom edge of the block, sticky side up.
- Place one of the folded pieces along the edge, folded side facing the pattern—overlapping 1/8 inch.
- Trim the ends.
- Repeat for all sides.

161

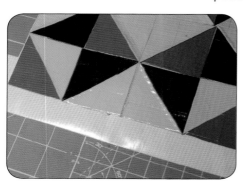

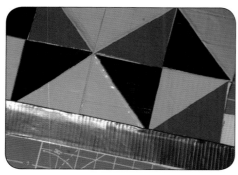

- Fold the remaining tape over, attaching the panel to the bag.
- Repeat on the three, non-zipper sides.
- Open the bag and stuff with packing peanuts, or other packing material (keeping in mind that some moisture could sneak in).
- Zip up the bag.
- Tape over the zipper edge as you did for the other sides.

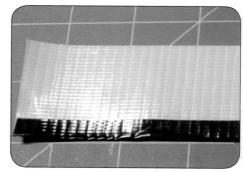

 ## Step 6: Attach. Stuff. Close.

The tricky part is over! You'll be relaxing in way more comfy lawn chairs in just a few minutes.

- Center the panel on the freezer bag.
- Unroll a 12" piece of tape (I used black for this part).
- Fold over about 0.25" of the tape.
- Lay tape on the panel, folded side towards the panel, overlapping with edging about 1/8 inch.

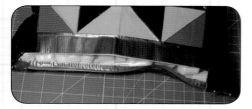

Milk Carton Planters

By Lauren Ryder
(annahowardshaw)
(http://www.instructables.com/id/
Duct-Tape-Milk-Carton-Planters/)

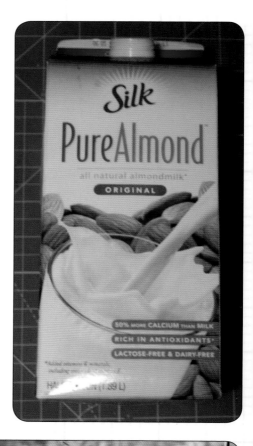

Why buy new planters like a sucker when you can quickly make more adorable ones from milk cartons and duct tape?

The combination of a waterproof carton and strong duct tape make these pots durable enough to use inside as well as outdoors.

Materials

- Milk carton
- Duct tape—gray, black, white, green, yellow, red Parchment paper

Tools

- Scissors
- Pencil
- Stencils (optional)

Step 1: Cut Milk Carton

- Get your milk carton (half-gallon or quart) and decide how tall you want your planter to be.
- Cut the top off the milk carton.
- Unfold the top piece.
- Remove the plastic spout.

Step 2: Cover Carton

- Cover carton in two layers of duct tape.
- Cut two 0.25" holes on opposite sides of the bottom of the carton.

  To ensure proper drainage, when you are ready to plant, fill the carton with gravel up past these holes. This will also prevent soil from running out.

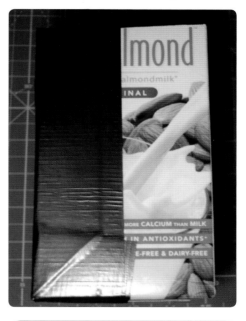

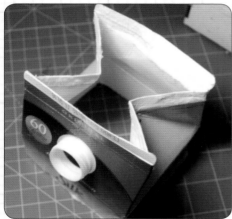

- Cut out the corners.
- Bend the sides.
- Tape the sides together.

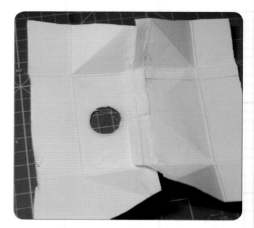

Step 3: Create Bottom Tray

The top of the carton is used to create the bottom tray for the planter.

- Cut the top piece in half.
- Lay the pieces out side to side.
- Tape the two pieces together.
- Place the carton on top of a piece to determine size—allow about a 0.5" all around to be turned up to make the sides.
- Cover the piece entirely in duct tape and fold up the sides.
- Make a 0.5" diagonal cut in each corner.

166

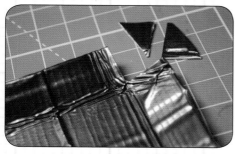

Step 4: Decorate!

Now the fun part! Using parchment paper allows you to create all kinds of duct tape stickers. You can make intricate designs without getting tape stuck all over the place or having it fold up on itself.

- Stick duct tape to the parchment paper
- Turn it over and, using a pencil, outline whatever design you'd like. You can use a homemade template from graph paper, a stencil, or just freehand drawings.
- Cut out your designs.
- Remove duct tape from the parchment.
- Affix your new decorations to the carton.
- Fill your personalized pots with plants and flowers.

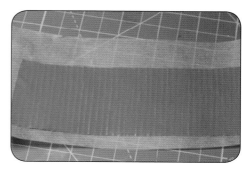

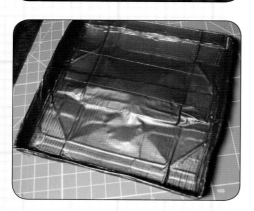

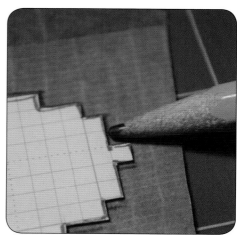

167

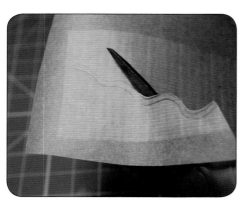

This duct tape waterproof pouch is sealed by doubled Ziploc bags under a quick release snap. Webbing on the back side allows for attachment to your life vest. Window cleaner helps make it possible.

You'll need

- Duct tape
- Window cleaner
- Scissors
- Razor blade
- Quick release snap
- Reflective tape
- Straight edge

Step 1: Setup

Find two Ziploc bags in the size you want to use. I used one-quart bags. Cut the bottom off of one of the bags. Place the intact bag into the bottomless bag. Adjust the bags so the zippers are one above the other. The zipper of the intact bag should be on bottom. See the pictures.

Spray your flat surface with window cleaner. Place the doubled bags on the wet surface and spray that as well. The window cleaner will give you some freedom in placing the tape. Don't worry, it will dry without affecting the performance of the tape.

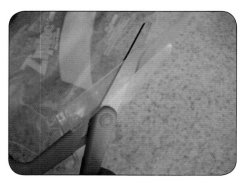

Step 2: Duct Tape Strips

Cut a strip of duct tape long enough to cover the width of the bag. Lay it over the bag and squeegee out any air bubbles and excess fluid. I'm using a Bondo plastic spatula, but a credit card works well too.

Continue overlapping strips until the entire bag is covered. Next, apply a layer of strips vertically. When that's done flip it over and do the same to the other side.

Apply cleaner as needed to keep it from sticking before you want it to.

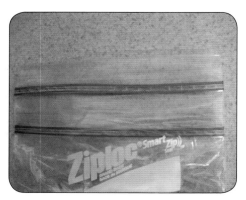

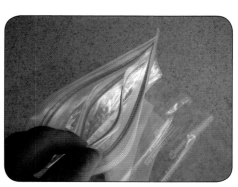

Place a couple of paper towels in it and let it dry over night. In the mean time, make the adjusting strap.

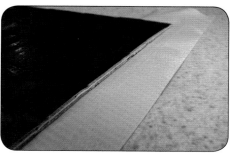

Step 3: Trim

Using a razor blade along a straight edge, remove the excess tape on the sides. Make sure to leave about 0.25" border around the Ziploc bag. You can overlay a third bag to help guide you.

Apply tape to the bottom and sides to cover the seams exposed from trimming. Also apply a single horizontal strip of tape over the Ziploc area to aid in pressing the zipper closed.

Wipe off any remaining window cleaner from the exterior of the pouch.

171

Step 4: Make the Adjusting Strap

Roll out a strip of tape long enough to wrap around the pouch twice. Generously spray it with cleaner and fold it in half. Align the edges before you squeegee out air bubbles and excess fluid.

Cut a strip from the tape in a width that corresponds to your quick-release snap. I have a one-inch snap so I cut a one-inch strip.

Feed the strip through the snap and secure one of the free ends by wrapping it with tape. Attach the strap with a couple of tape strips on the back side.

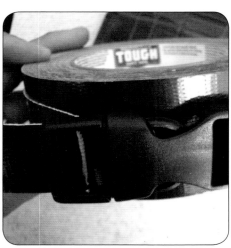

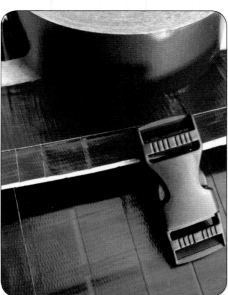

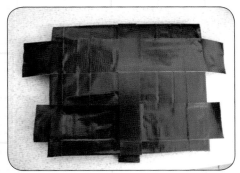

Step 5: Make the Webbing Loops

Measure out two sections of tape 5" long. Loop the tape around and attach it to itself. Keep the sticky side out.

Place both loops on the back side of the pouch and press them flat. Lay anther strip of tape over the loops to cover the exposed adhesive.

For looks, use scissors to round off the corners on the flap. You can also throw on some reflective tape.

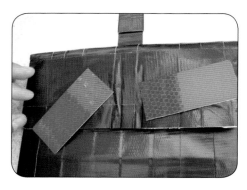

Step 6: Place It

Undo one of the straps on your life vest. Run the strap through the back webbing of the pouch. Re-do the strap and you're set. Now your secret map to the national treasure will stay dry.

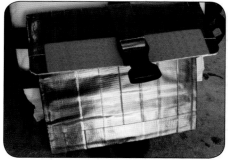

Section 6
Arts & Crafts

Realistic Rose

By Jason Poel Smith

(DIYHacksAndHowTos)

(http://www.instructables.com/
id/Realistic-Duct-Tape-Rose/)

This project is my attempt at creating a duct tape rose that is as realistic as possible.

Step 1: Materials

- Red duct tape (about 3–4 ft. per rose)
- Green duct tape (about 2–3 ft per rose)
- Red marker
- Green marker
- Floral wire (or other stiff wire) (about 10 ft)

Step 2: Making the Petals

To form the petals, start by cutting off a piece of wire that is about a foot long and a piece of red duct tape about 4" long. Stick the wire to the duct tape so that they overlap, about a third of the length of the duct tape. Then fold the duct tape over the end of the wire and stick the two sides together. This will form the basic structure of the petal. Cut the petal to shape by trimming the sides and rounding off the end. If you don't want the white adhesive to show, use the marker to color in the cut edges. Repeat

practical duct tape projects

this process for a total of ten petals. You will want to make a variety of sizes. In a real rose, the inner petals are smaller than the outer petals. Copying that structure helps you to get the shape right.

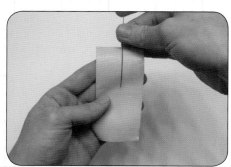

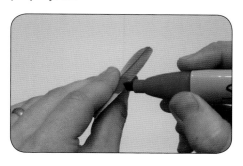

Step 3: Shaping the Petals

Start forming the rose by taking the smallest petal and loosely rolling it into a tube. Then, with each additional petal, there are few extra things that you need to do to shape them. Each petal should be offset from the previous one in a spiral. To make the petals gently curl around the center, pinch the tape as you wrap it. This makes the bottom of the petal a little narrower than the middle, making it a little more rounded. The rest of the shaping is done by bending the wire. Fold out the tip and press it toward the stem. This causes the middle to bulge and gives it its vertical curve.

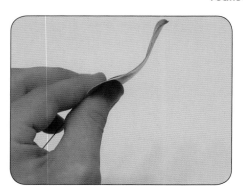

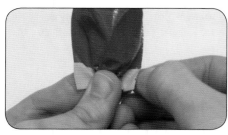

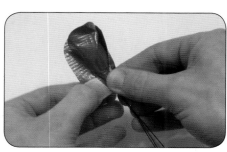

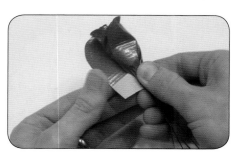

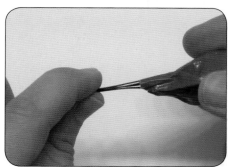

Step 4: Forming the Bud

Repeat the previous steps with each additional petal. After adding a petal, stop and make adjustments as needed. The final shape is determined by the kind of bud that you want to make. Younger buds have the petals more tightly wrapped and closer together. Mature buds are fuller and more spread out. It helps if you have a reference picture nearby while you are shaping the rose.

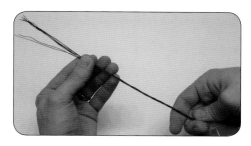

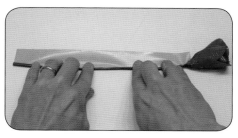

Step 6: Adding the Sepals

The last thing to add is the sepals. Cut off a 3" piece of green duct tape and fold one end over, similar to the way the petals were made. From this, cut out a small triangle with the exposed tape at the base. After coloring the edges with the green marker, attach it to the base of the flower. Repeat this for a total of five sepals. Try to keep them as evenly spaced as possible.

Step 5: Making the Stem

Once all the petals are attached, form the stem by tightly twisting all the wires together. To cover the stem, cut off a piece of green duct tape the same length as the exposed wire. Then roll the stem onto the duct tape. You may need to cut some slots in the top end to help it roll on straight.

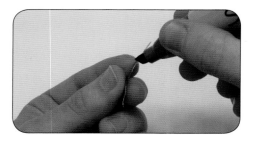

Step 7: Completed Rose

Do some final shaping and your duct tape rose is complete. Each rose will take about 30 minutes to make. So it is not a quick crafting project, but it is fun. You can use the basic principles to make other flowers as well. Experiment and try out different designs.

Lovely Lily

By Kate Newhall (knewhall)
**(http://www.instructables.com/
id/Duct-Tape-Lily/)**

This duct tape lily is a super simple variation on the classic duct tape rose. It's pretty simple, but a little messier than the very symmetrical rose design, as it requires gathering each of the petals as you attach them. It's okay if it looks a little rough as you assemble it, because the one of the last steps is to cover up all your folds with a single strip of long white tape that tightens and smoothes your petal layers.

Step 1: Gather Your Supplies

Colored duct tape (white, yellow, green)
- Wire coat hanger
- Scissors
- Wire cutters

Step 2: Make the Stem of the Flower

Using the coat hanger, cut a long and straight "stem" from one side of the hanger. Each coat hanger should make two stems.

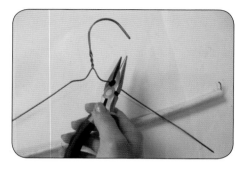

Step 3: Make the Inner "Pistil" of the Flower

Cut a 2" segment of yellow duct tape into two strips lengthwise. Repeat twice to make a total of three pistils. Save the fourth strip, unfolded. Fold the corners of each strip to make a point at each of the ends.

Step 4: Make the First Pistil

Take the first folded strip and wrap it around the wire stem to make the innermost pistil.

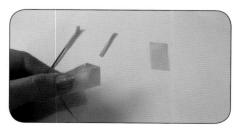

Step 5: Make and Attach Two More Pistils

Take the next two yellow strips (with pointed, folded ends) and wrap them around themselves, unattached to the flower. With the random fourth strip of yellow tape, attach the two pistils to the pistil anchored to the wire stem. You now have the center of your flower!

Step 6: Make the Petals of the Lily

Now it's time to make the white petals. Cut a 3" strip of white duct tape. Fold the corners lengthwise to make a wide point. Make sure to leave adequate tape exposed at the bottom to attach the petal to the stem. I like to make several petals at a time so that I can affix several in a row.

Step 7: Attach the Petals to the Stem

Using the exposed sticky tape, affix the petal to the stem, holding it at an angle. Gather the tape slightly as you wrap it around the stem so that it is a little loose and the petal stands up and out. Repeat this process several times with 4–5 more petals. You can stagger your petals up around on the back to make a more lily-like petal arrangement. Once you have added all the petals, cover up the gathers on the backside of the flower with a couple strips of white cut super thin.

Step 8: Color/Cover Your Stem

Now that all your petals are made, you will want to make your stem green by wrapping it in thin strips of green duct tape.

Step 9: Add Outer Leaves

Now that your flower is done, add green tape to make the outer green leaves. You will make these the exact same way you made the white petals.

Step 10: It's All Done!

A finished lily! It may not be perfect, but you get the idea. Mine tend to each turn out differently and I wind up using different numbers of petals depending on how the shape of the flower is coming along. After a few, you'll get a feel for where to stick each petal to build the shape that you want.

Duct Duck (Duck Tub Stopper)

By Kate Jackson
(shesparticular)
(http://www.instructables.com/
id/Duct-Duck-Duct-Tape-Duck-
Tub-Stopper/)

Duct tape is truly magical. It can be used for nearly everything, including creating an awesome little ducky which can then be attached to a tub stopper to make taking a bath super fun!

Step 1: You'll Need

- Duct tape (I'm using yellow, but you can use whatever color you like)
- Scissors
- Grommet tool and grommet
- Hole punch or leather punch
- Tub stopper
- Thin chain (approximately 10")
- Two coins or other small weights (I used pennies)
- Pliers (optional but suggested)

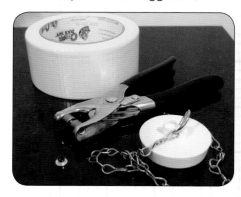

Step 2: Making Duct Tape Sheets

Before we can get to the folding process to create a duck, we'll need to make some duct tape sheets.

Cut a piece of duct tape approximately 9" long and place it sticky side up on your work surface. Cut two more pieces the same length and place them over the first so that they meet at its center. Flip the whole thing over and apply pieces to cover the outside edges. Repeat until you have roughly a square of duct tape sheet. Trim the sheet down to form an 8.5" × 8.5" square

Step 3: Get Ready to Spread Your Wings

Fold in two sides of the sheet to the center to form a kite shape. Then, fold the long point back to meet the shorter point. After that, fold the long point back again so that the fold is even with the layers underneath. Fold in the shorter point so that the tip meets the layers underneath. Then, fold the long point under itself to form a beak. When that's finished, lift the entire thing up and fold it in half to form two halves of a duck. Pull the neck and head portions out slightly and crease them into place. Fold the bottom portion on each side up to form the base of the body. Fold the flaps at the back of the body inside to form the tail portion. Position the coins under the body portion of the duck (on the inside) and cover each with a piece of tape. These will help ensure your ducky doesn't take a header when placed in water. Cut small pieces of tape and apply it to any areas that may need some help staying held together.

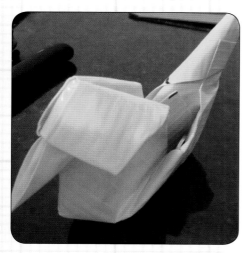

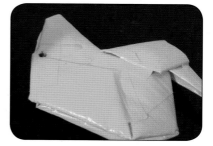

Step 4: Duct Duck . . . Goose?

You can skip this step if you just want to make a duct tape ducky, but making it into a bath stopper is even more fun!

Punch a hole in the back portion of the duck using a leather punch or hole punch. Using a grommet tool, add a grommet to the hole. Connect the duck to the tub stopper using the chain. Fill your tub, add bubbles, and hop in!

For a long time, I've wanted to make a duck out of duct tape. It's made out of newspaper, cardboard, dowels, a couple of black marbles, and lots and lots of tape.

I hung him in my office where he acts as my own personal attack duck to scare off my enemies. So far, everyone just says, "Aw, that's cute." They'll not think he's so cute once he pecks their eyes out.

Read on to see how to make your own!

Step 1: Body Base

For this project, I began by studying some photos of landing mallards. When I had a pretty good idea of what I wanted this to look like, I began the body by creating a bean shape out of newspaper and tape.

Sculpting with newspaper and masking tape is easier than you might think. You begin by just wadding up newspaper and wrapping tape around it. You can mold it into the shape you want by nipping and tucking the wad of paper together and putting tighter pieces of tape in place.

To add more material, you just tape on more wadded newspaper, and use a sharp knife to remove material. I've found that a heavy duty snap-style utility blade, with the blade extended and locked in place, works very well for carving and shaping.

Step 2: Body Shape Details

I added the neck, head, tail section, shoulder area, and leg nubs using the method described above—adding material and shaping it as needed.

Step 3: Body Modifications

Once the basic body shape was put together, modifications were made by slicing and carving with a utility knife and then re-taping everything back together.

As you work you have to constantly evaluate what you've got, and change it as you go. You can't be afraid to hack off a portion if it doesn't look the way you want.

Note the second photo—I had to do some drastic reconstruction to the head to acquire a decent duck-like head shape.

Step 4: Beak

The beak shape was made with cardboard that was hot glued in place. Newspaper was added with masking tape to fill out and finish the shape.

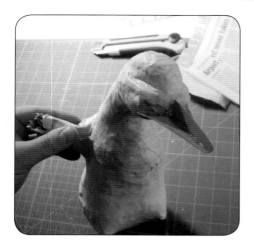

Step 5: Wings and Tail

The wings were started with newspaper and tape, and cardboard was added with hot glue to further develop the shape. A small cardboard tail section was also added.

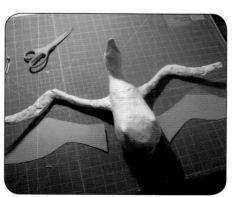

Step 6: Head Details

I used colored packing tape to cover the head. Black tape was used first and then covered with green. I tried a couple of other things, but I liked the way this looked the best based on what I had to work with. I used yellow electrical tape to cover the beak. Black marbles were glued into small holes cut into the head above the cheeks.

Step 7: Duct Tape Body Covering

I used white duct tape to cover the front half of the body and wings. Tail feather tips were cut with a utility knife.

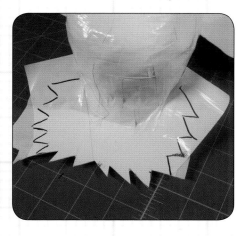

Step 8: Back and Chest Covering

Camouflage duct tape was used to cover the back of the bird's body and wings, along with the chest section. I think the camo makes it look really good.

Step 9: Wing and Tail Details

More colored duct tape was used to add the details to the back of the wings. The black tape is actually Gorilla Tape. After all the details were added, the feather-shapes in the wings were cut with a utility knife.

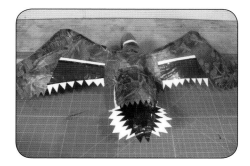

Step 10: Feet

Webbed feet were made with pieces of dowel and bamboo skewers covered with orange duct tape. These were glued into the little leg nubs that were sculpted into the body.

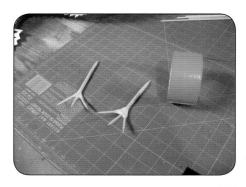

Step 11: Final Details

Simple details were added to the beak and toes with a black marker, and a screw eye was placed in the duck's back so it could be hung up.

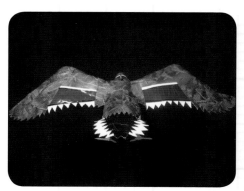

Masks

By Aaron Burrell (Silentz)
(http://www.instructables.com/
id/Duct-Tape-Masks/)

Okay, so you must have duct tape everything by now—duct tape shoes, socks, gloves, laptop bags, jackets, everything. But the one thing you don't have is a duct tape mask. The last bit of skin not yet covered by duct tape will be if you follow this.

It takes anywhere from 20 to 45 minutes, maybe more if you are a perfectionist. The white one in the photo below took an hour, because the shape of the muzzle/nose took a long time.

A lot of this Instructable is based on *your* imagination and designs, just to let you know.

Step 1: Materials and Tools

What you need

- Lots of cardboard
- Lots of duct tape (Colors you want your mask in)
- Masking tape

Tools

- Knife and/or scissors
- Cutting mat
- A pencil and a sharpie (or any other marking pen)

  Now you're set to make a mask!

Step 2: Designing the Mask

Basically, you've got to pick a shape of a head that you like. When you've found something that you like the look of, mess with the design a little more. (Although it might not be clear enough to understand what went on in my mind, a basic idea is shown below.) Remember to put eye holes in somewhere, and maybe even a mouth hole.

Step 3: Getting the Idea to 'Stick' Out

Next, we grab a piece of cardboard and the pencil. Freehand your design onto the cardboard lightly so you can make changes as you go, and make sure it is slightly larger than your head. Otherwise the mask won't make much of a mask and people will see the skin you want to cover! I would suggest splitting the design into two halves and drawing the two parts separate. That way, covering the card will be easier.

Once the design is down on card, cut it out using a knife and/or scissors and arrange the cardboard in the correct way. In this example, I have followed my original design from the paper in the last step. Do not worry about either side of the cardboard showing due to the fact of it will soon be covered in the duct tape.

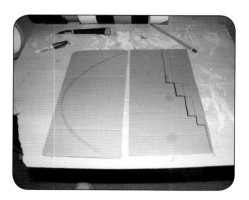

Step 4: Cover in Tape

The name of the step explains it all. Just grab the tape, cut to size, and lay it on. Once you have done both parts to the mask and you are happy, it's best to go over once more, just so the old cardboard color is completely covered.

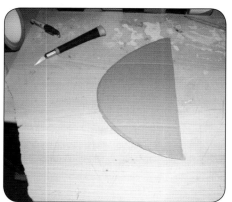

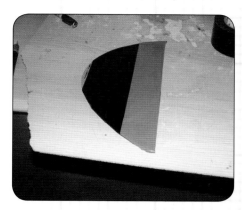

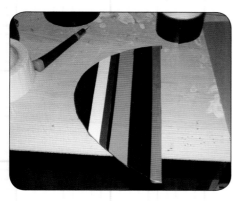

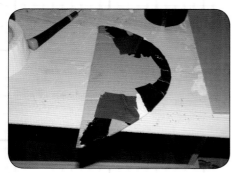

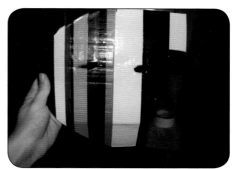

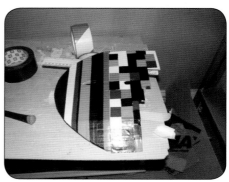

Step 5: Join the Two Sides as One

In this step, the idea is to create a spine or a kind of backbone made of normal tape or masking tape. Just follow the images below. Once the spine is created, use duct tape to cover. If on the front of the mask you don't have a problem covering the middle in tape, then do so. This just stops the mask from falling apart, basically.

Step 6: Finishing Touches

Now you can cover the back in duct tape to make it pleasing on both sides of the mask, and you can show it off when it's off your face.

You should also add a rubber band stapled to the mask, so you can wear it without holding it. I have no images of this however, as I don't do this to my masks.

Step 7: You're done!

Now go out into the big wide world with your duct tape face!

Tear-Away Scratch Pad

By wonderfulone
(http://www.instructables.com/
id/Duct-Tape-Tear-Away-Scratch-
Pad/)

Convert scrap paper into a handy notepad with tear-away sheets using duct tape instead of specialty binding glue.

What you'll need

- Scrap paper
- Cereal box or other cardboard for backing
- Duct tape
- Binder clips or rubber bands
- Glue stick
- Paper cutter
- Scissors

Step 1: Cut Your Paper and Backing

Using a paper cutter of your choice (swing arm, rotary, etc.), cut your scrap paper and backing to desired size. When you are stacking the paper after it is cut, be sure to stack so that the side to be bound consists of uncut edges. This step isn't absolutely necessary, but I have found that uncut edges are easier to align and adhere better. I chose to make mostly 5.5" × 8.5" and 5.5" × 4.25" notepads. I also made one 4" by 2.5" mini notepad. You can also leave the paper uncut if you prefer a full size scratch pad.

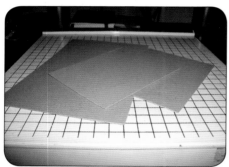

wrinkles and seep between the pages, causing them to stick together.

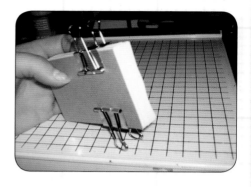

Step 3: Bind your Pages

Cut a length of tape slightly longer than the width of the edge to be bound. If you are making a notepad that is thicker than the width of your tape, use several strips positioned side by side. With the back of your notebook facing up, position the tape so there is enough overhang to cover the thickness of the pad. It is better to have too much overhang than too little, the excess can always be cut away. Press down on the backing to secure the tape, then flip the pad over. Starting from the middle, pull the tape upwards, while putting downward pressure on the pages, before smoothing the tape along the edge. Continue this motion outwards toward the edges until the width of the notebook has been secured with tape. Smooth down the taped edge, ensuring even adhesion. Cut way any excess tape.

Step 2: Prep your Pages

Once all your pages and backings are cut, align the edge to be bound until it is as smooth as possible. Any pages that are not aligned correctly will not adhere to the tape. Use binder clips or rubber bands to keep the pages and backing in place. Apply a thin layer of glue using a glue stick to help keep pages together while you apply the duct tape and to add a little extra stickiness. Do not use liquid glue; it will create

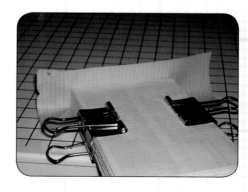

at least one straight side is possible (triangles, hearts). If you're particularly ambitious, you could try circles, stars, anything really

Before binding your pages, use a hole punch or a decorative punch to create an easy way to hang a scratch pad on a nail or thumb tack.

Print lines or a decorative header on pages before cutting and binding them, making your own custom stationary.

Apply a magnetic strip to the back of the scratch pad and hang it on the fridge for grocery lists.

Step 4: Other Ideas...

Rectangular or square notepads are easiest to make, but any shape with